Stephen Mason Merrill

Mary of Nazareth and her family

A Scripture study

Stephen Mason Merrill

Mary of Nazareth and her family
A Scripture study

ISBN/EAN: 9783337257736

Printed in Europe, USA, Canada, Australia, Japan

Cover: Foto ©Lupo / pixelio.de

More available books at **www.hansebooks.com**

MARY OF NAZARETH

AND HER FAMILY

A Scripture Study

By S. M. MERRILL, D. D.
BISHOP OF THE METHODIST EPISCOPAL CHURCH

CINCINNATI: CRANSTON & CURTS
NEW YORK: HUNT & EATON
1895

*COPYRIGHT
BY CRANSTON & CURTS,
1895.*

PREFACE.

THE genesis of this little book is this: While looking over some manuscripts of a book recently published, written by another, my attention was arrested by the statement of Neander, with regard to the question, "Who was James, the Lord's brother?" This venerable historian of the Church said: "This is the most difficult question in the apostolic history, and can not be considered as decided." The impression came to me that a little study might shed light upon this open question.

The doctrines involved are important, chiefly because of the use that has been made of unproved assumptions. In looking into it, the conclusion was soon reached that it is a question not to be settled by ecclesiastical history, but by the Scriptures alone. In this light it has been pursued, and as "a Scripture study" this little volume is sent forth, not so much as an exhaustive treatise, as an inquiry and a pointer in the right direction. It is believed that nothing essential to a right conclusion has been overlooked.

The temptation was strong to go into the history of the question to ascertain the opinions of "the fathers," and the beginnings of the controversy, as well as the growth and development of Mariolatry in the Roman Catholic Church, with its pernicious influence; but my preference for small books, and belief that the final authority must eventually prevail, determined me to adhere to the purpose to make it a "Scripture study."

The incidental matter of harmony between the evangelists is not the least important part of this investigation. The interpretation of Scripture by Scripture must not become a lost art. It is an exercise which always returns full compensation for the time and effort expended.

Whatever was critical in this study, requiring a look into the original, or a little tracing in etymology, has been given in result, without the processes of reasoning or the authorities relied upon. In the matter of names and words, the authorities are divided, so that the scope and connection of disputed terms is, after all, the only safe and final resort. If the conclusions here presented are sound, the reader will find, not only one, but several very difficult questions in apostolic history illuminated, if not settled. The relations of the Marys and the Jameses of the New Testament, and the questions with regard to the "brethren" of our Lord, must be questions of interest to all lovers of the Holy Scriptures.

S. M. M.

CHICAGO, February, 1895.

CONTENTS.

	PAGE.
CHAPTER I. THE SUBJECT STATED, ...	11
CHAPTER II. THE BIRTH OF JESUS, ...	26
CHAPTER III. HIS INFANCY—THE STAR AND THE MAGI, . .	48
CHAPTER IV. MARY, AND "THE OTHER MARY,"	71
CHAPTER V. HIS BRETHREN—CONJECTURES, ...	113
CHAPTER VI. HIS BRETHREN NOT DISCIPLES, ...	144
CHAPTER VII. HIS BRETHREN CONVERTED, ...	164
CHAPTER VIII. "THE LORD'S BROTHER,"	177

PROPOSITION.

Mary of Nazareth, the virgin mother of our Savior Jesus Christ, was the espoused wife of Joseph the Carpenter, who, under divine direction, took her under his protecting care till after she had brought forth her first-born son. She then, as his lawful wife, lived with him in the holy estate of matrimony, and bore unto him both sons and daughters, which sons and daughters were known to her neighbors and friends, and were acknowledged by herself and husband as their own, living in their house, and subject to their will. The names of the sons were James, Joses, Simon, and Judas, but the names of the daughters are unknown. These sons were known as the Brethren of Jesus, being the sons of his mother; but they did not become his disciples till after his crucifixion, death, and resurrection. They did, however, become identified with his followers before the day of Pentecost, and one of them subsequently became an apostle, known as "James the Lord's brother."

MARY OF NAZARETH.

Chapter I.

THE SUBJECT STATED.

THE first appearance of the name of Mary of Nazareth in Gospel history is in connection with her espousal to Joseph. It was undoubtedly by gracious design that the knowledge of her childhood and maiden life was withholden from the Church. In the early centuries there was manifested a disposition to magnify whatever was known of her into the supernatural, making it the occasion of undue veneration amounting to superstitious worship, such as is forbidden to any created being.

Whoever reads the brief story of her

call to the special mission assigned her, as the mother of our Savior, Jesus Christ, becomes deeply interested, and would love to know more of her than is possible. Curiosity in this respect can not be gratified. Only an occasional glimpse of her real life is all that is vouchsafed to us; but the little known of her is enough to call forth from all lovers of true womanhood the fullest sympathy with her cousin Elizabeth, when she said: "Blessed art thou among women!" While she is honored as the mother of our Lord, and held in highest esteem for her womanly virtues, there is no reason in her personal merits, or in her relation to humanity, for bestowing upon her divine honors, or for exalting her above her station as a person chosen of God for special service. Although honored as the instrument of special grace, she is honored only in her sphere as a woman meeting the providential requirement laid upon her.

In this relation to her mission, her virginity was an indispensable factor, fulfilling prophecy, and proving the divinity of her son; yet this holy estate, with the blessing of God upon it, was not in any sense a disparagement to marriage, which is an ordinance of God designed for the upbuilding of the race in all that makes existence a blessing. There is no law, human or divine, that condemns marriage, or makes motherhood a dishonor. It is never forbidden, except at the behest of priestcraft and superstition. God instituted the marriage relation at the beginning of human history, and ordained it for the race throughout all generations. "Marriage is honorable in all, and the bed undefiled." Hence, if it shall appear that Mary, after fulfilling her mission as the virgin mother of the incarnate Savior, fulfilled also the office of wife and mother, according to the order of God in developing his creative energy for the propagation of the race, not one ray of brilliancy shall be dimmed in the crown of her rejoicing. She is honored in every relation she sustained, in which she was obedient to the law of her being and the law of God.

The proposition laid down at the beginning of this treatise indicates the aim of all that is to be said. It is the conclusion reached after careful consideration of all the information available. The only authoritative record to be consulted is the Gospel history. Myths, legends, and traditions abound, but they are not to be regarded. If any allegation in this proposition falls short of support from the Sacred Scriptures, it must fall out of our conclusion, and by so much will this writing prove unsuccessful. If all are sustained, not the slightest shadow is cast upon the stainless reputation of the honored subject of this sketch. With all that is here attributed to her, she stands forth an example of purity and devotion, faithful in all her relations, obedient to the order of God, an ornament to her sex, and a benediction to mankind. Indeed it will appear, upon investigation, that the maintenance of all the allegations of this proposition is necessary to protect her from very serious implications—implications which involve her loyalty to her husband, and to the matrimonial vows which she assumed before the world in becoming a wife.

The scope of the inquiry to which our proposition leads is rather wide, not because of anything in the subject itself which is particularly difficult, but because of the denials and gratuitous assumptions made from time to time by those who have erected upon her brief history and special calling the marvelous system of creature-worship, not to say of idolatry, known as the Mariolatry of the Roman Catholic Church. It will not be necessary, fortunately, that we examine the growth and manifestations of that system, with its attendant superstitions, which have blinded and misled Romanists through generations past; but, since the foundation of the Romish errors is laid in the denial of the chief allegations of our proposition, the support of these allegations will leave the whole fabric of Mariolatry without anything to stand upon. "If the foundations be destroyed, what can even the righteous do?" The Christian intelligence of our times revolts at the extravagancies of Romanistic eulogies of the virtues of the "ever-blessed virgin," not because of any dislike to the due recognition of human excellence wherever found, but because it finds what is purely human exalted into the divine. The legends of superstition are held forth as revelations from God. The mother of the human nature of the Son of God is deified as the "Mother of God," as the "Queen of Heaven," and made the object of human and angelic worship. We stand aghast at this folly of the "Dark Ages," and yet find its influence wonderfully effective in holding the adherents of Rome to slavish obedience to priestly rule in this day of light, and in this land of liberty.

The traditions which have brought to our times the habit of attributing to Mary qualities unknown to herself and to the times in which she lived, and repugnant to the Holy Scriptures, when traced to their sources, betray an origin in the midst of the grossest darkness that ever settled on the Church; yet these traditions are not the subject of our study, nor in the range of our inquiry. Their falsity will be amply exposed in the light of the simple record of the life of Mary and her family, as given by the evangelists, when rightly interpreted. Our appeal is from the vain traditions of a superstitious age to the testimony of the writers of the New Testament. These are witnesses worthy of all credence. They wrote without bias, for the matters now in question were unknown to them. The disputes of later generations had not then arisen. Nor is their testimony conflicting when properly understood. Our business is to adjust the testimony so that one fact will shed light upon another, and so that what seems obscure will become clear when brought under the illumination of that which is too direct and plain to be misunderstood. We are to interpret Scripture by Scripture. In performing this task we are to remember that much of the material from which testimony is drawn relates to the subject in hand only incidentally, the main thought of the writer being quite aside from the issues pending. While these writers were alive such issues were impossible; for there could have been no question at that time about the family of the wife and mother, whose domestic relations have since then received so much attention.

Conditions arising from traditional expositions render it necessary to consider the relations of two families to one another, and to the apostleship as appointed or constituted by the Master when he first chose the twelve. The one family is that of Joseph and Mary, of Nazareth; and the other is that of Cleopas and Mary, whose residence is not given. In the family of Cleopas and Mary there were four sons, two of which became apostles—namely, James the Less, and his brother Judas; and our contention is, that there were also four sons, besides daughters, in the family of Joseph and Mary, which were not disciples till after the crucifixion. The coincidence—which is somewhat remarkable, and which has created confusion in the minds of expositors—is, that the four sons in each of these families bore the same names; that is, in both families were found James, Joses, Simon, and Judas, although there is no record of any sisters in the family of Cleopas and Mary. Whether these two families were related is a question. Mary seems to have been a favorite name in those days, as no less than five Marys are found among the women who had prominence in the apostolic record: First of all was Mary of Nazareth, the mother of Jesus; then, Mary, wife of Cleopas, and mother of James the Less; then, Mary of Magdala, who was healed of afflictions caused by demons; Mary of Bethany, sister to Martha and Lazarus; and Mary the mother of John, whose surname was Mark. The habit of naming children for relatives, so as to perpetuate family names, was so common as to be looked upon as a duty. When John the Baptist was born, the relatives wanted to give him the name borne by his father, Zacharias; and when his mother, Elizabeth, said his name should be John, as the angel of God had directed, the neighbors and cousins remonstrated, and said: "There is none of thy kindred called by this name." Hence, while the correspondence of the names of the sons in these two families indicates the possibility of relationship, it does not shed light upon the questions to be solved in the study now before us.

The real question is as to whether there were, in fact, two families of sons bearing the same names or not. In the interest of the Romanist doctrine of the perpetual virginity of Mary, the wife of Joseph, it is denied that she had any children other than her "first-born Son." In order to carry out this thought, it has been assumed and maintained with great vigor, so that many learned non-Romanists accept it, that the sons of "the other Mary" were members of the family of Joseph, being cousins to Jesus, and on this account called "his brethren."

In this interest it is also assumed that these two Marys were sisters; and that James the Less, and Judas, the brother of James, who were of "the twelve," and therefore disciples from very early in the public ministry of Christ, were of "his brethren," although not his brothers in any proper sense, or the sons of his mother. It is freely conceded that this hypothesis has the sanction of men of great worth and learning; that it is very old, probably dating from the third century; and that no particular heresy arises necessarily from its adoption, although it is necessary to the Romish dogma of the perpetual virginity, which is the basis of the whole scheme of Mariolatry. In other words, one might concede the identity of the sons of "the other Mary" with "his brethren" without accepting the notion of perpetual virginity; but this dogma of Rome can not possibly subsist without this assumption.

As intimated above, opinions on this subject of a divergent character were expressed at a very early period in the history of the Church. Citations from early writers, sufficient to give the scope of the discussions, would swell this treatise beyond its proposed limits, and yet fail to add to the light drawn from the Scriptures. Origen believed the persons called the brethren of Jesus were the sons of Joseph by a former wife. The dominant opinion in the Western Church was, that they were the sons of the other Mary; while that in the Eastern Church was favorable to the position of Origen. If the consensus of opinion at so early a day could be obtained, it would be influential; but that is impossible, since as little unanimity prevailed then as now. We must therefore proceed without bias from the expressed opinions of any writers outside of the New Testament. Modern commentators follow one another in a beaten track, with conjectures founded on very superficial study, as one may see by testing their reasons for the opinions preferred. Of course, it is seemingly presumptuous to speak with confidence where men eminent for learning speak tentatively, or without dogmatism; but it is to be remembered that most of those who have done so were absorbed with other great themes, and treated this subject as incidental. But few have given it direct and original investigation. When all of us have done our best, there will still remain some obscurities in the record, with regard to which hard questions may arise. It is not expected to remove all the difficulties which scholars have encountered for ages; but our utmost hope is to trace the facts given, so as to present conclusions in harmony with all that is written, consistent with themselves, and creditable to the character of the families most intimately concerned.

Chapter II.

THE BIRTH OF JESUS.

THE date of the birth of Jesus is not settled with absolute certainty. Matthew says: "In the days of Herod the king." This is not definite, nor was it the purpose of Matthew to make it so. The best authorities known place it in the fifth year before the era called *Anno Domini.* Luke tells us it was while Cyrenius was governor of Syria. This approximation to the date is sufficient.

The account given by Matthew of the marriage of Joseph and Mary, and of the birth of the child, is less minute than that given by Luke; but it has a different purpose. It is preparatory to the representation of prophecies fulfilled by the cruelty of Herod, and by the sojourn in Egypt. It is as follows: "Now the birth of Jesus Christ was on this wise: When as his mother Mary was espoused to Joseph, before they came together, she was found with child by the Holy Ghost. Then Joseph, her husband, being a just man, and not willing to make her a public example, was minded to put her away privily. But while he thought on these things, behold, the angel of the Lord appeared unto him in a dream, saying, Joseph, thou son of David, fear not to take unto thee Mary thy wife: for that which is conceived in her is of the Holy Ghost. And she shall bring forth a son, and thou shalt call his name Jesus: for he shall save his people from their sins. Now all this was done, that it might be fulfilled which was spoken of the Lord by the prophet, saying, Behold, a virgin shall be with child, and shall bring forth a son, and they shall call his name Emmanuel, which being interpreted is, God with us. Then Joseph, being raised from sleep, did as the angel of the Lord had bidden him, and took unto him his wife: and knew her not till she had brought forth her first-born son: and he called his name Jesus." (Matt. i, 18–26.)

This statement is designedly general; but it contains two expressions which are wonderfully expressive, and utterly irreconcilable with the notion that this babe was her only child. But the application is reserved till after the fuller account given by Luke is brought out.

"And it came to pass in those days that there went out a decree from Cæsar Augustus that all the world should be taxed. (And this taxing was first made when Cyrenius was governor of Syria.) And all went to be taxed, every one into his own city. And Joseph also went up from Galilee, out of the city of Nazareth, into Judea, unto the city of David, which is called Bethlehem (because he was of the house and lineage of David), to be taxed with Mary his espoused wife, being great with child. And so it was, that, while they were there, the days were accomplished that she should be delivered. And she brought forth her first-born son, and wrapped him in swaddling clothes, and laid him in a manger; because there was no room for them in the inn." (Luke ii, 1–7.)

Both Joseph and Mary were of the lineage of David. Two genealogies are given, one by Matthew and one by Luke; but they are not the same. It is thought by those who have most thoroughly investigated the questions raised by their divergences, that one is the line of Joseph's own descent, and the other that of Mary; but that, in that of Mary, the name of her husband is used as her official or legal representative. Mary was the espoused wife of Joseph. She took his name, and came under his lawful protection as a wife. Under divine direction, he took her, and gave her a home, and all needed care, shielding her person and her good name from the shadow of suspicion of evil till her first-born son was brought forth. A gracious providence guided her footsteps, and those of her husband, through all the trials her acceptance of the special mission from God brought to her. The formality of her marriage with Joseph is not given, but it was doubtless observed according to the custom of the times. It is enough for us to know that they became husband and wife.

This supernatural conception is reported without hesitation, and without any attempt at proof or explanation, as if the work of God needed no defense. It is plainly affirmed with sufficient circumstantiality, and left to vindicate itself in the life of the child born, the only proof tendered being the declaration that it was an event come to pass in fulfillment of prophecy. What God does is expected to commend itself to men who recognize his authority, without formal vindication. This is particularly so with miracles. Whenever any event comes into the range of human observation, bearing upon its face the appearance of the supernatural, being without conformity to the known laws of nature, it is proper and duty to study it in the character it assumes; and if it be found belonging to a class of events attributable to the immediate agency of God, the moral reasons for its occurrence are to be considered as the most weighty and as entitled to our highest respect. The absence of natural causes is not an obstacle to faith, where the moral reasons justify divine intervention, since dependence on natural causes would destroy the character of the event as a miracle. Supernatural events are not necessarily lawless; but their dependence is on forces or powers above the known laws of nature—upon something able to contravene or set aside known laws—although the superior power may be in strict accordance with the higher laws of the higher realm of God's great universe. In the material world it often happens that a known law of physics is arrested in its course by the intervention of a higher law, which is as natural as is the law arrested, when the superior prevails to the suspension or setting aside of the results which would naturally flow from the uninterrupted course of the inferior law. The higher law which is displayed in miraculous events, is something not definable, beyond the fact that it is the mode of the divine procedure, in the exercise of power beyond that contained in the system of nature which he has ordained. As he has not exhausted his resources by his investment in laws for the government of the natural world, we are not to deny the possibility of divine intervention for moral purposes where these subserve higher ends than can be reached by the orderly working of the forces known as natural laws.

God has often given children in answer to prayer. Isaac was born as one out of due time, a child of promise, involving the supernatural with scarcely less positiveness than did the birth of Jesus. Samuel was a son asked of the Lord, and granted to Hannah as a token of special favor. John the Baptist was the son of Elizabeth, born to her "who had been called barren," and by special promise and grace, when she was now "in her old age."

The supernatural birth of the son of Mary was in fulfillment of prophecy, one of the predictions of which is in Isaiah vii, 14: "Therefore the Lord himself shall give you a sign; Behold, a virgin shall conceive, and bear a son, and shall call his name Immanuel." Whatever local or metaphorical meaning this passage may have had in its primary and subordinate application to the rulers of Israel in the days of the prophet, it is enough for all the purposes of Christian faith to find the Evangelist giving it literal application to the child of Bethlehem. This is its literal meaning, its true and ultimate signification, whatever other events may have been embraced in the scope of its connections. This supernatural child was also the subject of another prediction by the same prophet: "Unto us a child is born, unto us a son is given: and the government shall be upon his shoulder: and his name shall be called Wonderful, Counsellor, The mighty God, The everlasting Father, The Prince of Peace. Of the increase of his government and peace there shall be no end, upon the throne of David, and upon his kingdom, to order it, and to establish it with judgment and with justice from henceforth even for ever. The zeal of the Lord of hosts will perform this." (Isaiah ix, 6, 7.) The Messianic character of this prophecy is unquestionable, except by the sheerest obstinacy in unbelief. It applies to no other. He is the supernatural child, the son given. While others have been born in answer to prayer, and have fulfilled providential missions, to the Son of Mary alone belongs the distinguishing honor of being "the only begotten of the Father, full of grace and truth."

Marvelous manifestations attended his birth, and sacred wonders crowded the days of his early childhood. The angel Gabriel visited the virgin chosen to be his mother, announced his coming, and pronounced her "blessed among women." Angels proclaimed his advent to the waiting shepherds, and filled the heavens with their chorus of praise. To the astonished watchers, who were terrified by the wonders they saw and heard, an angel spoke in assuring accents, saying: "Fear not: for, behold, I bring you good tidings of great joy, which shall be to all people. For unto you is born this day in the city of David a Savior, which is Christ the

Lord. And this shall be a sign unto you: Ye shall find the babe wrapped in swaddling clothes, lying in a manger. And suddenly there was with the angel a multitude of the heavenly host praising God, and saying, Glory to God in the highest, and on earth peace, goodwill toward men." (Luke ii, 9-14.)

No wonder that Mary "kept all these things, and pondered them in her heart." Filled with wonder, as she must have been, not the slightest incident could have been forgotten; and yet the future of the precious life committed to her keeping was graciously kept from her knowledge. It was not yet time for the iron to pierce her soul. Years of motherly anxiety were before her, with alternations of sunshine and shadow. From highest hopes, with unmistakable tokens of God's special favor and assurances of a divine mission for the child to fulfill, she was brought into humbling experiences of sorrowful privations, to grapple with distressing forebodings of impending evil. Steadfast trust in God, and silent submission, became the habit of her soul during the mysterious trial.

Loyal obedience to every requirement of Jewish law was promptly given. When that law directed circumcision, the child was circumcised; and when the time came for the mother's purification, and for presenting an offering for the child in the temple, not a jot of the law was disregarded. "And when eight days were accomplished for the circumcising of the child, his name was called Jesus, which was so named of the angel before he was conceived in the womb." Two lines of instruction were to be followed—that of the law, and that of the angel of God; but there is never conflict in divine requirements, and, therefore, these lines never clashed. God never, by any special revelation, leads any one away from the path of obedience to his law. The next step to be taken was to observe the requirement of the law concerning purification. This law is found in the twelfth chapter of Leviticus. Thirty-three days from the time of the circumcision of the child were required to fulfill it. At the end of that time, a lamb and a young pigeon, or a turtle-dove, must be "brought unto the door of the tabernacle of the congregation, unto the priest;" and if the person be unable to bring the lamb, then two turtledoves, or two young pigeons, will suffice. The mother must, therefore, remain at the place of the birth of the child till after it is forty days old. It was a long time for her and her husband to stay away from their home in Nazareth; but the law's demand was imperative, and impatience must not be indulged. It is not known whether room had been found in the inn for these strangers in Bethlehem, or whether they continued camping out, with the grotto-manger for their best shelter. The latter was most likely true. The weather was probably favorable for that kind of life, as it was at the season of the year when the shepherds kept their flocks in the open fields, which they did not do in the winter. Through the winter months, including December and March, they gathered sheep and cattle into the folds and under shelter; but in warm weather they left them out, themselves remaining with them during the night. While we can not fix the month in which the Savior was born, we can confidently infer that it was not in the winter, when the gathered flocks would leave as little room in the mangers as was in the inn. However this was, these parents tarried in Bethlehem till the forty days expired, when they started for their home in Galilee, prepared to stop in Jerusalem on their way to do for mother and child whatever the law required. Being in humble circumstances, they provided the offering which was acceptable from poor people—a pair of turtledoves, or two young pigeons. "And when the days of her purification according to the law of Moses were accomplished, they brought him to Jerusalem to present him to the Lord."

Here new surprises awaited them. There was nothing unusual in the offering brought, or in the ceremony performed by the priest; but other attending circumstances attested the Divine presence, and made the service memorable. Two venerable servants of God appeared in the temple at the time, who recognized the child as the Christ, and uttered words of blessing and prophecy, which filled the mother and Joseph with amazement. Only the inspired words can suitably represent the aged Simeon:

"And, behold, there was a man in Jerusalem, whose name was Simeon; and this man was righteous and devout, looking for the consolation of Israel: and the Holy Spirit was upon him. And it had been revealed unto him by the Holy Spirit, that he should not see death, before he had seen the Lord's Christ. And he came in the Spirit into the temple: and when the parents brought in the child Jesus, that they might do concerning him after the custom of the law, then he received him into his arms, and blessed God, and said,

Now lettest thou thy servant depart, O Lord,
According to thy word, in peace;
For mine eyes have seen thy salvation,

Which thou hast prepared before the face of all peoples;
A light for revelation to the Gentiles,
And the glory of thy people Israel.
And his father and his mother were marveling at the things which were spoken concerning him. And Simeon blessed them, and said unto Mary his mother, Behold, this child is set for the falling and rising up of many in Israel; and for a sign which is spoken against; yea, and a sword shall pierce through thine own soul, that thoughts out of many hearts may be revealed." (Luke ii, 25–35. Revised Version.)

Before their surprise at these marvelous words could find utterance, and before they could grasp their meaning, these parents were greeted by another venerable saint. "And there was one Anna, a prophetess, the daughter of Phanuel, of the tribe of Asher: she was of a great age, and had lived with a husband seven years from her virginity; and she was a widow of about fourscore and four years, which departed not from the temple, but served God with fastings and prayers night and day. And she coming in at that instant gave thanks likewise unto the Lord, and spake of him unto all them that looked for redemption in Jerusalem." Neither the exposition of the words of these aged servants of God, nor of their habits of worship in the temple, comes within the range of our purpose. We only note the fact that there were some in Jerusalem who were waiting for the consolation which only the coming of the Messiah could bring; and that the Spirit of God rested upon devout souls before the ushering in of the Spirit's special dispensation. In some way the Spirit of God revealed the presence of this Christ-child to these saints who looked for him, till their hearts glowed with celestial warmth, as they poured benedictions upon these parents, and upon the child, breathing the atmosphere of the border-land of heaven, and leaving no lack of proof of Divine inspiration.

"And when they had performed all things according to the law of the Lord, they returned into Galilee, to their own city Nazareth." (Luke ii, 39.) Such is the story of Luke. They were on their way home, and they made no needless delay. This is the fullest and most circumstantial account we have of the infancy of Jesus. It traces him from the manger in Bethlehem to his mother's home in Nazareth. It accounts for the providential presence of the parents at the place of his predicted birth; furnishes the data for ascertaining the time of this wonderful event; gives the par-

Chapter III.

HIS INFANCY—THE STAR AND THE MAGI.

WITH all the carefulness of Luke in tracing the early days of Jesus, from his birth to his first trip to his future home in Nazareth, nothing is said of the star in the East, the visit of the magi, the wrath of Herod, the flight into Egypt, the slaughter of the babes of Bethlehem, or the return from Egypt.

Luke purposely discontinues his narrative at the close of the ceremonies required by the law of Moses, when Joseph and Mary, with the child, took their departure from Jerusalem for Nazareth. This was the natural thing for them to do, under the circumstances. The supposition that they returned from Jerusalem to Bethlehem, and postponed their return to Galilee till after the flight to Egypt and return, is not only contrary to Luke's positive statement, but it is out of harmony with all the probabilities of the case, in view of their fixed residence in Nazareth, and of their hasty and temporary absence for enrollment.

There is evidently a long *hiatus* after the close of Luke's story, before he resumes it again, which Matthew fills with the incidents of the flight to Egypt; yet not so as to obviate questionings. When did the star appear? When did the magi arrive in Jerusalem? Whither did they go when they left Jerusalem? Where did they find the young child and his mother? These very natural questions can not be answered to the entire satisfaction of any one. Reasonable conjecture must be employed in order to the completion of any hypothesis one may adopt for the explanation of these wonderful incidents, as related without date or chronological order by the first evangelist.

Skeptical writers have taken advantage of the manifest incorrectness of the popular belief with regard to the time of the appearance of the star, and the visit of the magi, and the flight to Egypt, and have alleged positive and irreconcilable contradictions between Matthew and Luke touching the early days of the young child's life. It is held that the story of the "wise men" was legendary or mythical, akin to the stories of the apocryphal Gospels, unknown to Luke, unrecognized by any other writer, and unworthy of belief. It is true that Luke makes no mention of it; but it is not true that he leaves no room for the events it describes. It is also claimed that Matthew was equally ignorant of the visit to

HIS INFANCY. 51

the temple, and of the testimony to the child's future, given by the aged Simeon and Anna. Of course, when properly interpreted, there is no contradiction between these evangelists; but one supplements the other. Luke tells nothing that took place after the child was taken from the temple; and what Matthew relates must have occurred after that time. The whole story of the star and the magi and the flight into Egypt is not to be rejected because there is no room for these things between the birth of the child and the return to Nazareth. If Matthew placed all these occurrences inside of the first forty days of the child's life, there would be difficulty in harmonizing the two writers; but he does not.

It is not to be denied that the popular impression is at fault. If we undertake to find the magi in Bethlehem before the child was taken home to Nazareth, by the way of the temple, failure is unavoidable; and yet this is the commonly-accepted view. Evidently it is the idea followed by artists and poets. The pictures represent the magi as opening their treasures and presenting their gifts to the child in the manger, in the presence of the "beasts of the stall;" and some of the most beautiful songs ever sung describe the magi as following the star to the "manger-bed." It seems a pity to interfere with the poetic license which allows these inaccuracies; but these pictures and songs create the popular impression which opens the way for the cold criticisms of the unbelieving; and neither the songs nor the pictures are of any value in comparison with the consistency of the Gospel narratives.

The account given by Matthew is as follows: "Now when Jesus was born in Bethlehem of Judea, in the days of

Herod the king, behold, there came wise men from the East to Jerusalem, saying, Where is he that is born king of the Jews? for we have seen his star in the East, and are come to worship him. When Herod the king heard these things, he was troubled, and all Jerusalem with him. And when he had gathered all the chief priests and scribes of the people together, he demanded of them where Christ should be born. And they said unto him, In Bethlehem of Judea: for thus it is written by the prophet, And thou Bethlehem, in the land of Judah, art not the least among the princes of Judah: for out of thee shall come a governor, who shall rule my people Israel. Then Herod, when he had privily called the wise men, inquired of them diligently what time the star appeared. And he sent them to Bethlehem, and said, Go, search diligently for the young child: and when ye have found him, bring me word again, that I may come and worship him also. When they had heard the king they departed; and, lo, the star, which they saw in the east, went before them, till it came and stood over where the young child was. When they saw the star, they rejoiced with exceeding great joy. And when they were come into the house, they saw the young child with Mary his mother, and fell down and worshiped him: and when they had opened their treasures, they presented unto him gifts, gold, and frankincense, and myrrh. And being warned of God in a dream that they should not return to Herod, they departed into their own country another way. And when they were departed, behold, the angel of the Lord appeareth to Joseph in a dream, saying, Arise, and take the young child and his mother, and flee into Egypt, and be thou there until I bring thee word: for Herod will seek the young child to destroy him. When he arose, he took the young child and his mother by night, and departed into Egypt, and was there until the death of Herod: that it might be fulfilled which was spoken of the Lord by the prophet, saying, Out of Egypt have I called my son. Then Herod, when he saw that he was mocked of the wise men, was exceeding wroth, and sent forth, and slew all the children that were in Bethlehem, and in all the coasts thereof, from two years old and under, according to the time which he had diligently inquired of the wise men. Then was fulfilled that which was spoken by Jeremy the prophet, saying, In Rama was there a voice heard, lamentation, and weeping, and great mourning,

Rachel weeping for her children, and would not be comforted, because they were not." (Matt. ii, 1–18.)

Assuming the truth of this narrative, the first thing to do, in order to bring it into line with the description of the events of the early days of the young child's life as given by Luke, is to find out, if possible, the time of this remarkable visit of the "wise men," and of the sensation produced in Jerusalem by their visit. There is evidently too much of it to have occurred within the forty days before the presentation in the temple; and since Luke so closely follows the child up to that time, he certainly would not have omitted all allusion to these events if they had come within the period of his narrative.

But judgment must finally be based on what Matthew says, rather than upon what Luke does not say. Why, then was this visit to Bethlehem impossible before the child was taken away? It is generally conceded that the magi came from Persia. They are understood to have been Chaldean astrologers, learned in the wisdom of the Orient, and men of wealth and dignity. Such men moved deliberately, and never with haste. After observing the star and studying its import, they considered the journey, and made preparation for it. It is not probable that they started for some weeks, and possibly months, after the star appeared. Their journey would occupy several weeks after it was begun. Their speediest transportation was by camels. Then they tarried in Jerusalem till they could interview Herod, and till the chief priests and scribes could search the Sacred Writings, and report to the king a conclusion with regard to the place where the Messiah should be born. Before all this could be accomplished, the "forty days" were expired, and Jesus had been presented in the temple, after which ceremony, Luke says, "they returned into Galilee, to their own city Nazareth."

The record itself will not permit the supposition that the magi appeared upon the scene in Bethlehem before the presentation in the temple. The reason is—and it is commanding—that immediately after the departure of the magi to their own country, Joseph took the young child and his mother, by night, with every appearance of haste, and departed into Egypt. There was no such thing as the presentation of the child in the temple, with the impressive occurrences which Luke records in connection with that service, after the wise men had disappointed Herod, and after Joseph had been warned of God in a dream to "flee into Egypt." After that warning,

Joseph made no public appearance in Jerusalem with the child and his mother, but without delay sought safety by carrying the child beyond the reach of Herod's power. This settles the question beyond dispute as to the non-appearance of the magi between the birth of the child and the return to Nazareth.

The popular impression, carried out in art and in song, is, that the wise men not only went to Bethlehem and found the child, but that they found him "in the manger," the place of his birth. But the words of Matthew do not authorize this impression. Indeed, it is an utterly groundless impression, contrary to the language of the record. "And when they were come into the house, they saw the young child with Mary his mother." Whether the "house" they were in was their own house in their own city of Nazareth—whither they had gone—or not, is not so material at this point; but it is certain they were "in the house," and not yet in the place of his birth, where he was laid in the manger.

It is not denied that the account as given by Matthew wears upon its face an appearance as if the magi went from Jerusalem to Bethlehem, and there found the babe. It is not strange that such is the popular belief. After consulting the priests and scribes, Herod "sent them to Bethlehem." They followed his advice so far as to start in that direction. The journey was easily made; two hours would accomplish it. If they were going the right way, with a plain road before them, and almost in sight of their destination, why should the star again appear to guide them? There has always been strict economy in supernatural manifestations, when the end was possible by natural means. These men were following not only the instruction of the king, but that of prophetic inspiration as well. They were going to Bethlehem, as they had been told in Jerusalem, to make inquiry for the child, whose appearance had not been a secret, but was known to the shepherds, and perhaps to the populace. Additional miraculous intervention can scarcely be accounted for, if they were in the way to find the object of their search. They were little more than out sight of Jerusalem before Bethlehem would come into view. Why, then, should the star appear? Was it really needed? The words of Matthew neither say, nor do they necessarily mean, that the star led the wise men to Bethlehem. It intercepted them in their course, and such was their joy on seeing it that the instruction of Herod was no longer regarded, unless it agreed with the leading of the star. "And, lo, the star which they saw in the east, went before them, till it came and stood over where the young child was." Not over the manger, nor necessarily over any house in Bethlehem, but "over where the young child was." According to Luke's account, he had been taken to the temple before this, and with his mother and Joseph "to their own city Nazareth."

"The star went before them." This sounds as if they were following it in a way that they knew not. Possibly it guided them during the night till they found their devious way around Jerusalem to the north of the city, in the direction to Nazareth, "where the young child was." Much traveling was done in the night in that climate, and perchance these star-led travelers spent more than one night in their journey to the place where the star rested. Indeed, the intimation is rather plain that they did; for they must have slept on the way after they left Jerusalem, which they would not do in going to Bethlehem, because they dreamed, and were warned of God in their dream not to return to Herod. If this be conjecture, it is in the line of harmony in the Gospel narratives. Something of the kind is necessary to this end; for the account given by Luke, which so definitely fixes dates, and traces the child so carefully, requires some draft upon the imagination to provide for this visit of the magi at all, while there is not a word in the story of Matthew inconsistent with it.

After they had found the place, and "were come into the house," they made their prostrations as in the presence of royalty, and then opened their treasures and made their presents. This done, "they departed into their own country, another way." Their obligation to Herod was no longer upon them, since his instructions did not lead them to the child. From Nazareth they could easily do this, as they were very nearly on the line to Damascus, or to any main route to Persia; while from Bethlehem the natural way would be through Jerusalem, although they could find a difficult line eastward by way of the Dead Sea and the fords of the Jordan.

Immediately after this visit of the magi, the flight into Egypt began. There was no reason for delay, other than hasty preparation for the trip, as all the requirements of the law of Moses concerning the mother and child had been met. He had been circumcised on the eighth day, and he had been presented to the Lord in the temple, and the proper offering had been made for him when forty days old, so that no ceremonial duty remained unfulfilled. His parents were at liberty to go with him beyond the jurisdiction of Herod, without violating any law. They started by night. It was probably more comfortable to travel by night than by day. The journey to Egypt is not described. It is thought the sojourn there lasted nearly two years. Traditions respecting the life of this family in Egypt are not trustworthy. They were hidden from view for a time, and all conjectures concerning their doings or experiences are vain.

When Herod found that the magi would not return to him, his anger burned. He felt that he had been "mocked" and cruelly deceived. His kingly pride was wounded, and his malicious design upon the life of the "young child" seemed thwarted. This he determined should not be. He would destroy the possible aspirant to the throne if it cost the life of every child in Bethlehem. "Then Herod, when he saw that he was mocked of the wise men, was exceeding wroth, and he sent forth and slew all the children that were in Bethlehem, and in all the coasts thereof, from two years old and under, according to the time which he had diligently inquired of the wise men." The crime of murder was not new to Herod, but the cruelty of this slaughter has been seldom equaled in the history of human atrocities. It is thought that not less than forty innocents fell victims to his inhuman rage, which is not an extravagant estimate.

There is an objection to the thought here advanced, that Jesus had already gone from Bethlehem before the wise men appeared, on the ground that if he was safe at home in Nazareth, there would have been no need of the flight from there to Egypt, in order to escape the danger at Bethlehem. This is the most plausible objection to the chronological order herein favored, that has been made, or that seems possible; and yet it is inconclusive. If safety were certain at Nazareth, the flight to Egypt was unnecessary, even from Bethlehem; for in that case all that was needed was that Joseph and Mary abandon any thought they might have been cherishing of adopting Bethlehem as their home, and return to their own city and home in Nazareth. If there was safety there from Herod's persecutions on one hypothesis, there was also on the other. God's thought was, that the child should be removed out of Herod's jurisdiction. He must therefore leave Galilee as well as Judea, as it is not likely that all the danger was in the neighborhood of Bethlehem.

There is also a note of time in this report of Herod's rage, which is of value in judging of the period of the visit of the magi. When they first came to Jerusalem to make inquiry concerning the child, Herod inquired of them "diligently," or very particularly, what time the star appeared. He sought to know the age of the child at that time. Then, after their departure, when he found they did not return, he issued the decree for the destruction of the children "from two years old and under, according to the time he had diligently inquired of the wise men." He estimated the age of the child from the time of the appearance of the star, as he had learned it from his strange visitors. It is clear that only a little time elapsed after they left Herod, till he knew they had left the country, perhaps a few weeks, and probably not a month; and yet he included the children "two years old" in his decree of death. Of course, this estimate of time can not be taken as exact, since the cruel king would allow a margin, so as to make sure of his intended victim; but if the star appeared one year before the decree of death to the children, it would still bring the wise men to Jerusalem, and to Bethlehem, if they went to Bethlehem, some time after the presentation in the temple and the return to Nazareth. It can scarcely be possible, in the light of all the facts, that the wise men found the child before he was six months old; and yet the consecutive and minutely definite story of Luke takes the mother and child away from Bethlehem at the end of the days of her purification according to the law of Moses, and presents him in the temple while on the way home; showing that, in the natural order of things, they would reach Nazareth in less than fifty days after the child was born.

Many writers pass over this matter as of little importance, simply assuming that the wise men found the babe in Bethlehem, without suspecting any difficulty in harmonizing the accounts of Matthew and Luke. This is unfortunate, and inexcusable, indeed, in any who pretend to accuracy. Others see the difficulty in adjusting the chronological order of events, so as to make room for the visit of the magi in Bethlehem, and assume that Joseph and Mary returned to Bethlehem, after the presentation in the temple. If it were absolutely necessary to locate the visit of the wise men in Bethlehem, in order to meet the language of Matthew, a return trip would have to be assumed. It is, however, the height of folly to think of the presentation in the temple as occurring after the wise men had been there and departed. Then, if the wise men found the child in Bethlehem at all, it was after the presentation, and there must have been a return trip after leaving the temple, either before or after the return to Nazareth. Matthew mentions their "turning aside" to dwell at Nazareth, as an afterthought; but that was not till after the return from Egypt. Then they went to Nazareth, that being out of the jurisdiction of Archelaus, the kingdom of Herod being divided on his death; Archelaus reigning in Judea, and his half-brother becoming tetrarch of Galilee. The sojourn in Egypt had broken up their home and loosened their ties in Nazareth, so that it is not strange that they now thought of taking up their abode in the city of David, where Joseph was enrolled, and where the child was born, whose birth had given such distinct intimations that he was destined to sit upon the throne of David, to order and rule the kingdom of Israel. There was a Providence which directed the steps of those to whom was committed the charge of this young child; and Providence never favored any thought Joseph and Mary might have entertained of bringing up this child in Bethlehem. It would have been inconsistent with the experiences they had been through, for them to plan to live in Bethlehem without some intimation of the Divine will; and it does not accord with any right conceptions of God's dealings with this family to suppose that they were divinely led to leave their home in Nazareth, and transfer all their interests to Bethlehem, just a few days or weeks before the necessity would be upon them to move on to Egypt. This thought appears legitimate, and it antagonizes the supposition of any return to Bethlehem after the presentation in the temple, or after the return to Nazareth, before starting to Egypt.

Writers sometimes remind us that we often find events mentioned in the Scriptures as if they were closely connected in time, when in fact they are separated by months and years. There are examples of this kind that might be cited; and so it is held that the return to Nazareth mentioned by Luke, may not have occurred immediately when they left the temple, as the language seems to imply, but might have followed the sojourn in Egypt, and be the same trip described or mentioned by Matthew. To this view there are strong objections. If the description of the child-life of Jesus, found in Luke, were as general as is the language of Matthew, there would be more reason for taking this supposition as probable; but there is evident exactness in Luke's narrative, as far as he carries it, which is to the point of the departure of the family for their home in Nazareth. Luke did not mention the visit of the magi, for the reason that his plan did not carry the story of the child to the time of its occurrence. The same is true of the flight to Egypt. He only followed the movements of the family till the requirements of the law were fulfilled, when they all started back to Galilee. His is a Judean history of the child. What occurred in the family, or happened to the child in Galilee or in Egypt is passed over by

HIS INFANCY. 75

him till the child and his mother again appear in Judea, and are found in the temple. He left the family when they left the temple, and he resumed his narrative when the family returned with the child, now twelve years old. The whole story of Matthew relates to events between these two points. When Luke resumed, and related the second temple scene, wherein the child of twelve displayed such wisdom in the presence of the "doctors," he described only what occurred on that one occasion, and spoke of the return of the family again to Nazareth, where the child remained subject to his parents; and then he broke off the narrative as before till the appearace of John the Baptist, whose office it was to introduce the public ministry of Christ.

When Joseph and Mary left Nazareth before going to Egypt, whether they first went to Bethlehem or not, they evidently broke up their residence, so that when the sojourn in Egypt was over they contemplated taking up their abode in Judea. It was natural that they should think of this, since they must have regarded the future of the child, which was their special charge, as related to the metropolis of the Jewish people, so as to make it proper that he should grow up in that vicinity. It was not, therefore, their first thought to return to Nazareth; but while hesitating because of their fear of Archelaus, the voice of warning in a dream determined them. It was evidently not the Divine purpose that they should reside in Bethlehem, and there is doubt whether they ever saw the city of David, the birthplace of Jesus, after they closed their temporary visit, and took the young child to the temple, when forty days old, on their way to their home in Nazareth, which they had temporarily left for the purpose of enrollment. Since there is no mention in the Scriptures of any return to Bethlehem, either from Jerusalem or from Nazareth; and since there is nothing in the words of Matthew which necessarily takes the wise men into Bethlehem when they started to go there; and since it is plain that the sudden reappearance of the star, when they were approaching the suburbs of that city, intercepted them for a purpose, and caused them to disregard the instructions received in Jerusalem; and since the star "went before them," and they followed it, not to the manger, but "till it came and stood over where the young child was;" and since the wise men first saw the young child with Mary his mother "when they were come into the house;" and since they had been sleeping and dreaming after seeing the star, the implication is very strong that they found Mary and the child in their own house, in their own city, Nazareth. With this order of events there is not the slightest disagreement between Matthew and Luke, nor is there occasion to assume a return trip to Bethlehem, which is neither asserted nor hinted at in the Scriptures.

If we must assume that there was a return to Bethlehem; and if we must find the magi in that city; and if we must believe that the star reappeared to guide them where they were really going, and when they were nearly there,—then, by all means, let the assumption be that the parents went from the temple to Nazareth, as Luke affirms, and that the unrecorded return was from Nazareth to Bethlehem. The assumption in this form will not contradict either of the evangelists, and as it is only an assumption, it will encounter nothing worse than the implication that the parents gave up their home in Nazareth, and removed to Bethlehem, on their own motion, without consulting providential indications, since all these point to Nazareth, and not to Bethlehem, as the child's providential home. It is always difficult to reach conclusions on historical points in the absence of testimony, yet it is sometimes necessary to form theories in order to supply omissions in the record. Well for us, if in emergencies requiring this, we do not substitute mere guesses for rational inferences. It is particularly true, and should not be astonishing, that when the supernatural works with the natural forces of life in bringing about a providential purpose, unexpected turns "surprise" us, even to our bewilderment. The teachable spirit is therefore becoming when we study the brief outlines given us of the history of the child-life of the son of Mary. God was with him, and watchful love guarded his steps in every movement from his birth in Bethlehem till his mission was crowned with triumph in his ascension from Olivet to his Father's throne.

Chapter IV.

MARY, AND "THE OTHER MARY."

SINCE the aim of this treatise is more than biographical, its design can be best accomplished without attempting to restrict the treatment of facts recorded to the chronological order, even if such an order were possible. Beyond the events making up the history, it looks to the solution of the most difficult problems which have arisen in connection with the brief record we have of this extraordinary Galilean family. The chief question calling for attention has come down to us from an early period in the history of the Church, not later than the third century, and has to do with far-reaching influences in the Christian world. It is as to whether any other ing when we study the brief outlines given us of the history of the child-life of the son of Mary. God was with him, and watchful love guarded his steps in every movement from his birth in Bethlehem till his mission was crowned with triumph in his ascension from Olivet to his Father's throne.

Chapter IV.

MARY, AND "THE OTHER MARY."

SINCE the aim of this treatise is more than biographical, its design can be best accomplished without attempting to restrict the treatment of facts recorded to the chronological order, even if such an order were possible. Beyond the events making up the history, it looks to the solution of the most difficult problems which have arisen in connection with the brief record we have of this extraordinary Galilean family. The chief question calling for attention has come down to us from an early period in the history of the Church, not later than the third century, and has to do with far-reaching influences in the Christian world. It is as to whether any other child than Jesus was born into this family. A very simple question, indeed, it appears to be at first blush; but around it have raged some of the most acrimonious and persistent discussions of Christendom, and upon a single view of it have been founded some of the most powerful institutions of the Church of Rome. The doctrine of the perpetual virginity of the mother of Jesus has long been vital to that Church, as upon it rests the whole system of Mariolatry or creature-worship, which has been the source of so much superstition and spiritual blindness among Romanists for ages.

In our present study of the subject, it is not in our thought to undertake the impossible task of filling up the long period of silence which the Scriptures leave, no doubt providentially, with regard to this family, extending from the time Jesus was twelve years old, till he was about thirty; for there are no data, either in the sacred writings, or in any other writings, to guide in such an effort. It was, perhaps, according to the purpose of God, that nothing should be told us concerning Joseph and Mary during this time. Their domestic life does not seem to have been designed for public observation any more than the private affairs of any other family, except when it had some special significance in connection with the life of Jesus, the firstborn son of Mary. The later allusions to the family indicate to us nothing from which we can infer anything other than that they lived a quiet and honorable life, awaiting providential developments with regard to Jesus, and properly caring for the other children which Providence gave them. It is remarkable that in all the Scriptural allusions to this family, Jesus is always the central figure. Mary appears always as "his mother," and the other children are mentioned as "his brethren," and "his sisters." Whatever is said of these is incidental, and comes out only as it relates to him and his work.

This brings us to the great fact in question. There was a family in Nazareth, of which Joseph and Mary were the head, in which Jesus lived as a son, and was known as such to all the neighbors; and in which there were other children known as his brothers and sisters. This fact is well attested, being recognized by all the evangelists. So far as appearances go, there was nothing extraordinary in the constitution or composition of this family. The husband and wife were lawfully married, and their occupation was creditable. They were of the industrial class, and probably shrank from notoriety, although they were well aware that in their household was one destined in some way to accomplish an extraordinary mission.

The presumption is, that the brothers and sisters in this family were what the language so clearly means—the sons and daughters of Joseph and Mary, and "his brethren" and "his sisters." There was certainly no law against the existence of such a family, and nothing discreditable to any of the parties. Motherhood was not then dishonorable. Indeed it was the glory of womanhood. It is inconceivable how the idea originated that perpetual virginity could honor the name of Mary. She had honored the period of her virginity, and entered the estate of matrimony so as to honor that by living the life of a loyal wife, and becoming a loving, faithful mother. The assumption that she could or did at the same time observe the vows of *celibacy* and of *matrimony* is absurd. No accurate writer would speak of her son as "her firstborn son," if there were not others born to her at a later period. Not only is the implication of this expression clear and unmistakable, but the other children are found and known by name.

Not only was Jesus called "her firstborn son"—implying that others were born later—but the limit to the period of her virginity is distinctly marked in the declaration concerning her marriage. Joseph took his "espoused wife," and yet as a wife he "knew her not *until*—" If she never became a wife, what language is this? It is not merely meaningless, but it is misleading and false. It stamps the transaction with fraud. She pretended to what was unreal, unnatural, deceptive, and fraudulent. Why it should be deemed a glory to her, or be taken as an evidence of sanctity, to live in such a false relation, is most wonderful. The consensus of virtuous womanhood is against it.

Joseph and Mary have been accused with indifference, or with lack of parental watchfulness, on the occasion of their "first-born son's" appearance in the temple when but twelve years old. They started on the homeward journey without looking after him. They thought he was in the company; but they did not know, till they had gone a day's journey, that he was not among his "kinsfolk and acquaintance." Then, of course, their anxiety was aroused. Careful parents, with so tender a charge, would not have been so easy about him, unless they were occupied with the care of younger children. In that event, their conduct was natural, and free from blameworthiness. On any other supposition, it is hard to excuse them, or to free them from the charge of neglect. It is not said that younger children were with them; but this supposition is not to their discredit, and it is the best vindication of their course that can be devised. If there were younger children, the boy of twelve would have acquired some experience and confidence in looking out for himself.

There is another side to this representation of the family of Joseph and Mary, of course, or the great discussions of past centuries would not have taken place. In those discussions almost every phase of the question has been canvassed, and several different hypotheses have been set forth to account for the existence of a family of children in the house of Joseph and Mary, known as the brothers and sisters of Jesus, without allowing them to be such in fact. The different explanations offered must not be disregarded, but whatever of merit or plausibility there is in them must be brought out.

The study of these hypotheses will lead to an inquiry concerning another Mary, known in the Scriptures as the wife of Cleopas, the mother of James the Less, and frequently mentioned as "the other Mary." This Mary seems to have had sons bearing the same names as "the brethren of Jesus," on which account many have taken her sons to be the ones the Scriptures call "his brethren." To give color to this supposition, the very remarkable claim has been set up that these two Marys were sisters; and some have gone so far as to hold that they were both widows, living together in Nazareth as one family, where the children of "the other Mary," were taken by the neighbors to be the brothers and sisters of Jesus. The theory is, that they were not his brothers in the sense of being the sons of his mother, but only "cousins"—the word brethren being used in so general a sense as to denote relatives, without regard to the degree of kinship. Of course, the word "brethren" is used sometimes to indicate a fellowship in a common cause or work, but only when its metaphorical use or meaning is apparent. When used to express blood kinship, its literal meaning must prevail, unless a different meaning is not only obvious, but necessary. When the angel spoke to Mary of her relative, the wife of Zacharias, who was to be the mother of John the Baptist, he said: "Thy cousin Elizabeth." The word "brother," or "brethren," is as definite in the Greek of the New Testament as with us; so, also, is the word "cousin." These words are not synonymous, nor are they used indifferently. Neither of the evangelists said "brethren" when "cousins" were meant.

There is, however, no available proof that the children of this "other Mary" were the cousins of our Lord. It is not conceded that the two Marys were sisters. So remarkable a thing as two sisters in the same family bearing the same name is not to be accepted without the most indubitable and explicit testimony. It is too unusual, if not preposterous, to be received on slight ground. No evangelist asserts it; no properly-read passage hints it, or implies it; and no alleged fact requires it to be taken as an inference. It is simply a mistake. The only basis for it is a single verse in John's Gospel, which is misread and misinterpreted when that meaning is given to it. The slight ambiguity in one verse, the real meaning of which is easily gained, is quite too narrow a foundation for an hypothesis of such extraordinary character to rest upon. We must study the passage, and see the unreasonableness of the construction which makes sisters of the two Marys.

There is something peculiar in this matter of kinship with Jesus. He had many "kinsfolk" among whom he might have traveled from Jerusalem on the occasion of his visit to that city when twelve years old. He had two "cousins" in the apostleship from the beginning, without regarding James the Less as one. The fact has not been so generally recognized, but is nevertheless pretty clearly established, that the mother of Zebedee's children was sister to Mary, the mother of Jesus, and that she was the "sister" who was present with her at the cross. Hence it follows that James and John, the sons of Zebedee, were his cousins. The proof of this is much more satisfactory than anything that can be said in favor of the proposition that James the Less sustained that relation to him. In fact, there is no available proof at all on this point, notwithstanding the confidence with which the assertion has been made, and its wide acceptance.

This study of the kinship of Jesus with the apostles brings up another question which must receive due attention, because it is vital in the main issue. The Apostle Paul, in speaking of his early association with the apostles after his conversion, says: "Then, after three years, I went up to Jerusalem to see Peter, and abode with him fifteen days. But other of the apostles saw I none, save James, the Lord's brother." (Gal. i, 18, 19.) What James was this? Why was he called "the Lord's brother?"

The position of those who deny that the Lord had any brother is well understood, but must be stated again. It is, that this James was "James the Less," one of the twelve, who was the son of Alpheus, and whose mother was Mary, the wife of Cleopas, the alleged sister to Mary, the mother of Jesus; and that being a cousin to Jesus, he was called his brother, in a sort of loose or general use of the word. Everything in this view of the case hinges on the unproved assumption that these two Marys were sisters. Whether there was a third James, who became an apostle, as did Paul and Barnabas and others, who were not of the twelve, is also involved in this inquiry. If the two Marys were not sisters, the children of "the other Mary" were not cousins to Jesus—not on his mother's side, at least—and therefore James the Less could not have been called the "Lord's brother" on the ground alleged, meaning not brother, but cousin. Thus it appears that so much depends on proving the extraordinary proposition that two sisters in the same family were named Mary, that one might properly expect the proof to be as clear as the sun in a cloudless sky; but, instead, it does not amount to proof at all, being only an improper reading or punctuation of a sentence in a single verse.

The passage which means so much in this discussion is John xix, 25: "Now there stood by the cross of Jesus, his mother, and his mother's sister, Mary the wife of Cleopas, and Mary Magdalene." The meaning of this verse very largely depends on the tone and punctuation. It can be read so as to favor the hypothesis which makes the two Marys sisters; but that is evidently not the true meaning. The question is, How many persons, besides the mother of Jesus, were designated as standing by the cross? If only two, then one of them was his mother's sister, and that one was named Mary, the wife of Cleopas. But if there were three women designated, then "his mother's sister" was not named by John, and was not the wife of Cleopas. It is easy to read the passage so as to indicate the presence of three in addition to "his mother," and thus bring it into harmony with the statements of the other evangelists on the same point, who clearly mention three. Let it be read with a different punctuation, so as to bring out the sense: "Now there stood by the cross of Jesus, his mother and his mother's sister; Mary, the wife of Cleopas, and Mary Magdalene." Since punctuation is not of divine authority, that is best which best gives the sense of the writer. The two sisters are properly joined in one member of the sentence. Then the third one of the group is "Mary, the wife of Cleopas." The occurrence of the semi-colon at once distinguishes the persons as not the same, and supersedes the conjunction "and," which might have been used without altering the sense. The conjunction between the words "sister" and "Mary" would certainly have necessitated the meaning here contended for; and yet it was not necessary to express that meaning, because the person named after "sister" was not the last one named in the list. It is common usage, and good usage both in Greek and English, to omit the conjunction till the last name in a list is reached, or till the beginning of the last member of a compound sentence. Peter, James, and John is the common form. But where two are related, or more intimately grouped than others, it is good form to join them in one expression, as "his mother and his mother's sister;" and, while the semicolon here would better bring out the sense, neither its absence, nor the absence of the conjunction "and," binds us to accept a meaning which is so unusual and extraordinary as that sought to be put upon this verse. Learned essays have been written to show that the absence of the "and" (*kai*) in this place proves the strange assumption not hinted at elsewhere in all the Scriptures, that the two Marys were sisters, and that only two women were designated by John as standing with the mother of Jesus at his cross. But all the other evangelists designate three, while the best reading of this passage, either with or without the better punctuation, clearly indicates three. His mother's sister, who was not named, was the first; Mary, the wife of Cleopas, the second; and Mary Magdalene was the third.

In confirmation of this reading, we shall find out that these three were present; and we shall also find the name of this sister to the mother of Jesus, whom this evangelist did not name; and we shall find, in addition, the reason why John did not give her name; and also that she was John's own mother. If all this be shown, then, of course, the other interpretation which makes the two Marys sisters fails of proof, and goes down with all the vast superstructure of Mariolatry and false interpretations built upon it. A most marvelous instance is this of almost infinite results following a mistaken reading of a single verse—nay, a single sentence in a single verse!

The record by the other evangelists

settles the question as to the number of women present—that is, the number of those designated, and, inferentially, as to the one who was "sister" to the mother of Jesus. We read, Matthew xxvii, 55, 56: "And many women were there beholding afar off, which followed Jesus from Galilee, ministering unto him: among which was Mary Magdalene, and Mary the mother of James and Joses, and the mother of Zebedee's children." Here are the three who were sufficiently prominent or important to be designated particularly, as those who came with Jesus from Galilee, ministering unto him. There is no reason to doubt that Matthew and John designated the *same three* who were with the mother of Jesus, although Matthew does not mention her as present at all. Of these three, two are the same that John named, and the third is the one whom John did not name, but mentioned as sister to Mary, the mother of Jesus. She is not named here, but is identified as "the mother of Zebedee's children." She is, therefore, the mother of James and John. Now, by turning to Mark xv, 40, 41, we find the same group recognized and designated as follows: "There were also women looking on afar off: among whom was Mary Magdalene, and Mary the mother of James the Less and of Joses, and Salome; who also, when he was in Galilee, followed him, and ministered unto him; and many other women which came up with him unto Jerusalem." All the three which are honored with such particular mention were with him in Galilee, and followed him, and ministered unto him, a service in which Salome was conspicuous. Mary Magdalene, and "the other Mary," the mother of James the Less, are never omitted. The third of this select group is named by Mark, but otherwise designated by Matthew and John. Matthew calls her "the mother of Zebedee's children;" John speaks of her as the sister of the mother of Jesus—"his mother and his mother's sister;" but here in Mark she is "Salome." Collating all these, we designate her at once as Salome, sister to Mary the mother of Jesus, wife of Zebedee, and the mother of James and John. She was with Jesus in Galilee, and ministered unto him, probably furnishing him with a home much of the time he spent in Capernaum and the vicinity of the lake, before his mother moved from Nazareth, and possibly after she and her other children came to Capernaum to live. She certainly came with him from Galilee up to Jerusalem; for it was on this journey that she brought her two sons to Jesus, and requested him to place them, one on his right hand and the other on his left hand, when he should come into his kingdom. A very strange and bold request, one is ready to say, and utterly presumptuous, till we remember the relation she sustained to Jesus, as his mother's sister, and his own aunt and hostess, and as the mother of two of his most devoted and most beloved disciples, who were with her, and joined her in the request.

John was peculiar about mentioning the names of those especially dear to him. Among these were his mother and the mother of Jesus. These are not named in his Gospel. His brother James he does not name. All these are recognized in his writings, so as to be identified, but not by name. It was so with his own name. When he spoke of himself, it was "that other disciple," or the "disciple whom Jesus loved," or "the disciple which testifieth of these things." When he spoke of his brother and himself, he said, "the sons of Zebedee." When he spoke of Mary, the mother of Jesus, the name was omitted, and it was "the mother of Jesus," or "his mother." So when he would identify the two women at the cross of Jesus for whom he felt the tenderest sympathy and the deepest veneration, he wrote, "His mother and his mother's sister." There must have been in his nature some peculiar sensitiveness on this subject, perhaps a feeling akin to that which restrained a devout Israelite from pronouncing the name of the Deity without uncovering his head. Now, in view of this singularity in John's character, it appears in exact keeping with his method, to indicate the presence of these two sisters in this way, without naming either, or intimating the relation of either to himself. His own mother, "the mother of Zebedee's children," was one of the most prominent of the noted women who ministered to Jesus in Galilee, and who came up to the feast, and stood by the cross. She was conspicuous in every good work, and was not absent when the supreme trial came. True to her faith, and true to her instincts of sisterhood, she was with the mother of Jesus in this darkest hour, and with her till after the Sabbath was past, and with those who brought the glad news of the resurrection on the morning of the first day of the week.

John named the other women without hesitation. He said, "Mary the wife of Cleopas;" that is, literally, "Mary of Cleopas," the word "wife" being supplied, where the word "daughter" might have been inserted; or, if *Klopas* were a place, and not a person, it would be Mary of *Klopas*, as Mary Magdalene is Mary of Magdala. But no such place is known, and Clopas, or Cleopas, is the name of a person, and the indication of this Mary as his wife is probably correct. It seems to have been another name for Alpheus, it being not unusual for one to be known by two names, as Matthew was also Levi; and as Bartholomew was also Nathanael; and as Simon was called Cephas; and as Lebbeus was Thaddeus, and possibly Judas.

When Luke made reference to the women standing at the cross, he did it in a more general way. He gave no names, simply saying: "And all his acquaintance, and the women that followed him from Galilee, stood afar off, beholding these things." But further along in the story, when he describes the fidelity of those who remained till after the burial, and prepared for the embalming, he gives the names of the women who reported the resurrection, and among them one who was not of the distinguished group that stood afar off, witnessing the crucifixion. She may have been present, as were many others, but she was not spoken of by name, or in any way designated till after the resurrection. She can not therefore be thought of as being the unnamed "sister" to the mother of Jesus; nor yet as the "mother of Zebedee's children." The identification of that one already made can not be impeached. Luke says: "It was Mary Magdalene, and Joanna, and Mary the mother of James, and other women that were with them, which told these things unto the apostles." (Luke xxiv, 10.) Joanna was undoubtedly a person of some importance, worthy of this mention in this company of excellent women, whose names are enshrined forever in the hearts of believers, as well as written in the imperishable records of inspiration. If unknown in all other relations, this one recognition would place her among the honorable women whose devotion led them early to the forsaken tomb, and brought them visions of angels, and made them the first witnesses of the resurrection of the Son of God. She was, by implication, one of those of whom this evangelist says: "And the women also, which came with him from Galilee, followed after, and beheld the sepulcher, and how his body was laid. And they returned, and prepared spices and ointments; and rested the Sabbath day according to the commandment." These same women, after the Sabbath, while it was yet twilight, on the morning of the first day of the week, came to the sepulcher, to carry out their purpose of embalming the body, when, to their great astonishment, they found the stone rolled away, and the sepulcher empty. Their distress at this discovery was at first agonizing, but it lasted only for a moment; for just then appeared angels from heaven, and announced to them the most stupendous fact in the history of Redemption. "He is not here; for he is risen, as he said." Then immediately one of the angels, to quiet the alarm of the women, that they might assure themselves of the reality of the wonderful things taking place before their eyes, tenderly said to them: "Come, see the place where the Lord lay." He then bade them go and tell his disciples that He who was crucified was risen. Luke says it was "Mary Magdalene, and Joanna, and Mary the mother of James, and other women that were with them, which told these things unto the apostles." Mark puts John's mother, Salome, among them: "And when the Sabbath was past, Mary Magdalene, Mary the mother of James, and Salome, had bought sweet spices, that they might come and anoint him. And very early in the morning, the first day of the week, they came unto the sepulcher at the rising of the sun." John does not include his mother in the list of these early visitors, but she was there, as she was never behind in the ministry of love. Mary the mother of Jesus was not there. She remained alone in her silent grief, or perhaps with her other sons, whose fidelity to her never failed, while kindred and friends from Galilee attended to the kindly offices for the dead. But here we find the name of this other woman, Joanna.

Who, then, was Joanna? May it not

be, after all, that this is the unnamed sister to the mother of Jesus, who stood with her at the cross? We find her name elsewhere among those who had received healing at the hand of Jesus. "And it came to pass afterward, that he went throughout every city and village, preaching and showing the glad tidings of the kingdom of God; and the twelve were with him. And certain women which had been healed of evil spirits and infirmities, Mary called Magdalene, out of whom went seven devils, and Joanna the wife of Chuza, Herod's steward, and Susanna, and many others, which ministered to him of their substance." (Luke viii, 1-3.) Joanna is thus identified. She was the wife of Chuza, Herod's steward. Her devotion to Jesus was like that of Mary Magdalene, a tribute of gratitude for personal healing. She was not mentioned as standing at the cross, but she was probably there as one of the other women. She was not the unnamed sister, to whom John referred. (John xix, 25.) That was Salome, "the mother of Zebedee's children." Thus every line of investigation brings us back to the inevitable conclusion that three women stood with the mother of Jesus at his cross, and that these three were Salome, his mother's sister; Mary the wife of Cleopas; and Mary Magdalene. This fact is far-reaching in this discussion, and tells with tremendous power against the unnatural supposition that Mary the wife of Cleopas, was the sister of Mary the mother of Jesus. It also applies with equal decisiveness against the claim set up that James the Less, was the apostle whom Paul designated as "James the Lord's brother."

Chapter V.

HIS BRETHREN—CONJECTURES.

IN order to do full justice to the hypothesis which denies to Jesus any brother, and to his mother any other child than her "first-born son," we must look at the several conjectures put forth to give it the appearance of plausibility. If the hypothesis be sustained, it must, in some reasonable way, account for all the facts known to exist in connection with this family in Nazareth.

The leading fact, which is palpable and indisputable, is, that there was a family of children living in the house with Joseph and Mary, as if they belonged there, and known to the neighbors as their own. Unless this can be explained in harmony with the supposed non-parentage of this husband and wife, the hypothesis falls to the ground for want of support. Hence the ingenuity of believers in the perpetual virginity has been taxed to the utmost to give a plausible solution of the problem. The result is, that the ground is taken that these children were all the children of another Mary, who, upon the slender ground already considered, is alleged to have been the sister of Mary the wife of Joseph, making her children cousins to Jesus, and on that account called his brethren. It is also assumed, on this behalf, that Joseph was dead, and that Cleopas, the husband of "the other Mary," was dead; and that these two widowed sisters, both named Mary, were living together in one house, as one family, and that the neighbors who knew Jesus, looked upon the other children in this household as his brothers and sisters, when, in fact, they were only his cousins.

The ingenuity of this conjecture is not questioned; but its foundation has already been removed in the showing that there is not the least shadow of reason for believing that these two Marys were sisters, or ever lived together as one family. The children of this family were not only supposed by the neighbors to be the brethren and sisters of Jesus, but the "brethren" are recognized by the sacred writers themselves as "his brethren," again and again, and that through all his ministry and till after the crucifixion and the Pentecost. Moreover, they are spoken of as "his brethren" in his presence, and without any denial or modification on his part. Further than this it is scarcely necessary to go; and yet, in order that the entire lack of trustworthiness in this conjecture may appear, it will be shown that facts do not admit of the supposition that either one of these Marys was a widow at the time these children were living in the family and passing in the community as the brothers and sisters of Jesus. It is a sort of common tradition that Joseph died before Jesus began his public life, but there is no proof of it; and it is simply a part of the conjecture which seems necessary to the dogma involved, and which is so essential to Roman Catholicism — the Mariolatry of that Church resting upon it.

There is not the least particle of proof that either Joseph or Cleopas was dead. The occurrences which bring these children into view belong to the earlier part of the public ministry of Jesus. He had been baptized; he had been through the temptation in the mountain or wilderness; and had returned to Nazareth, where he preached in the synagogue, and astonished the people, so that they said: "Is not this the carpenter's son? is not his mother called Mary? and his brethren, James, and Joses, and Simon, and Judas? And his sisters, are they not all with us? Whence, then, hath this man all these things?" This familiar way of alluding to Joseph as "the carpenter," who was well known, and whose sons and daughters were at home, is not the way they would have spoken if "the carpenter" had been dead. The implication is clear that the whole family lived there, so as to be known by name. At a later period in his ministry, when Jesus had come over to Capernaum from beyond the lake, and, in addressing the people, had spoken of himself as "the bread of life," and as "the bread which cometh down from heaven," "the

Jews murmured at him, because he said, I am the bread which came down from heaven. And they said, Is not this Jesus, the son of Joseph, whose father and mother we know? how is it then that he saith, I came down from heaven?" It is unreasonable to imagine the people thus speaking if his "father and mother" were not both living. His mother was, we know, and the two are so associated in the minds of those who spoke of them as to imply that they were together. It is not at all likely that they would have spoken of Joseph in this familiar way if he had been dead. They did not refer to him as one dead, or as having once been known to them, but as still living, "whose father and mother we know." In this way people speak of their acquaintances who are living. The whole tenor of the Scriptures is against the supposition that Joseph was dead at the time James and Joses and Simon and Judas were at home in Nazareth, known as the brethren of Jesus, and as the children of Joseph and Mary. We may safely set this conjecture aside, not merely as not proven, but as proven false. It is not known when Joseph died; but evidently it was not before the time when the murmuring Jews said: "His father and mother we know." The probability is that Joseph lived till near the close of the public ministry of Christ. The fact that he was not recognized as being present at the crucifixion, and that after that the mother of Jesus was put under the care of her nephew John, who took her to "his own home," to live with his mother, who was her own sister, gives color to the supposition that her husband was dead at that time. This presumption of her widowhood at the time of the crucifixion proves nothing favorable to the conjecture that she had been a widow for a long time, and had been living with a sister whose children passed for her own. If that had been the case, there appears no particular reason for breaking up so delightful an arrangement by sending her to live elsewhere. But if her husband had recently died; and if her home in Nazareth had been broken up but a short time; and if she had lately gone to Capernaum to reside; and if "the mother of Zebedee's children" was really her sister, who did the sister's part by standing with her at the cross; and seeing that her own sons were not yet disciples, and were not settled for living or for business,—the arrangement for her was natural, and can be easily understood. The mother of James and John was evidently in good circumstances. Zebedee was possibly still alive. The home was one where Jesus and his mother were not strangers, and where the kindly attentions of the "beloved disciple" would come to her as a balm to her wounded spirit. In all probability, the commendation of Jesus to his mother and John, to regard each other with motherly and filial love, did not change the home which had previously opened to her; but sanctioned and sanctified an order of things which was now to become permanent, and needed only his blessing.

The conjecture before us makes "the other Mary" a widow also, living in Nazareth with the mother of Jesus, where her children were taken to be the brothers and sisters of Jesus. What ground is there for supposing she was a widow? Not the least in the world. It is gratuitous guess-work, pure and simple. Moreover, it is highly improbable. She is not at any time spoken of as a widow, but always as a wife. She is the wife of Cleopas. If Cleopas was living when she was mentioned as being his wife, she was identified at once. The question as to whether Cleopas and Alpheus are identical, is not involved at this point, but simply the question as to whether Mary, the mother of James the Less, was the wife, or the widow, of Cleopas. She is called his wife; but is there any ground for believing him dead? There certainly is not; while all references to him, and to Mary his wife, clearly imply that he was living. This ought to be sufficient to set aside a baseless conjecture; but, then, there is proof on the other side. Cleopas was living, and he was a disciple, probably known to all the company of the disciples gathered at Jerusalem; a witness of the crucifixion, and one to whom Jesus revealed himself after his resurrection. He was one of the two disciples walking towards Emmaus, when the risen Christ came to them, and walked and talked with them, and then made himself known to them. We read, Luke xxiv, 13-18: "And, behold, two of them went that same day to a village called Emmaus, which was from Jerusalem about threescore furlongs. And they talked together of all these things which had happened. And it came to pass that, while they communed together and reasoned, Jesus himself drew near, and went with them. But their eyes were holden, that they should not know him. And he said unto them, What manner of communications are these that ye have one to another, as ye walk, and are sad? And the one of them whose name was Cleopas, answering, said unto him, Art thou only a stranger in Jerusalem, and hast not known the things which are come to pass there in these days?" Here is a disciple named Cleopas, and he is evidently one of the "acquaintances" who lingered about the cross till all was over, and then remained with the sorrowing company till the Sabbath was past. He identified himself with those most intimately concerned, when he said: "Yea, and certain women also of our company made us astonished, which were early at the sepulcher; and when they found not his body, they came, saying that they had also seen a vision of angels, which said that he was alive. And certain of them which were with us went to the sepulcher, and found it even so as the women had said." (Luke xxiv, 22–24.) The women who went first to the sepulcher were "of our company;" they also "made us astonished;" and, then, "certain of them which were with us went to the sepulcher." Surely, then, this disciple was with the apostles, and with the women, and there is no reason for doubting that he was the Cleopas who was the husband of "the other Mary," one of the women last at the cross and first at the sepulcher; and this Mary was the mother of James the Less, one of the twelve. It is therefore impossible that she should have been a widow, living in Nazareth with the mother of Jesus, and her children passing as the brethren of Jesus. At that very time two of her children were apostles, traveling about with Jesus in the active pursuit of his great mission. Thus it appears that this conjecture of the widowhood of these two Marys is contradicted by facts too formidable to be set aside without positive testimony, which is wholly lacking and impossible.

Commentators follow one another in the hasty conclusion that this Cleopas, whom Jesus met on the way to Emmaus, is not the same as the husband of Mary. There is a slight difference in the orthography of the name in different places; but, unless the derivation is proven to be entirely different, this fact proves nothing. Whether written Clopas, Cleopas, or Cleophas, there is not the shadow of argument against the identity of the person in the spelling, since very many proper names in the Gospels are differently spelled. Even Simon is sometimes Simeon. (Acts xv, 14.) No other Cleopas than the husband of Mary is known to have been so intimately related to the disciples as this man is shown to have been; and if he were another, the fact would have been intimated in some way.

There is still another conjecture to be considered. Some who concede that there were two families with sons of the same names, assume that those passing as the brothers of Jesus were the sons of Joseph by a former wife, and were, therefore, his stepbrothers, and popularly known as his brethren in the community. The age of this conjecture, though it be traced to the second century, gives it no authority. While it is more plausible than is the assumption that the two Marys were sisters, it is without the semblance of truth, having no recognition in the Scriptures. No one knows whether Joseph was a widower or not, whether he was an elderly man or quite young, when he married Mary. The work of artists in representing him as an old man is purely imaginary. It is like that of picturing the mother of Zebedee's children as a beautiful young woman, with two little boys at her knees, asking Jesus to place one of them at his right hand and one at his left, in his kingdom; when, in fact, this request was made in behalf of two apostles, of full stature and mature life. If Joseph had been married previously, and had these four sons and several daughters, even the youngest of them would have been older than Mary's "first-born son," and some of them considerably older; and as Jesus was thirty when he began his ministry, some of them would have been settled in families of their own, and would not have been living with their stepmother, and accompanying her from place to place as her children, subject to her will, while Jesus was going about with his disciples preaching the Kingdom of God.

While we may not deny the possibility that Joseph was a widower, the conjecture is devoid of important elements of probability. It is in the highest degree improbable that he had a family of children at home, and left them to care for themselves, when he so hastily took Mary and the young child and departed into Egypt. While they were older than the child whose life he sought to save, they were not at that time—thirty years before the beginning of Christ's ministry—old enough to warrant the father and stepmother in departing out of the country without making provision for their protection and support. It is next to impossible to believe that any humane father would do such a thing, or be providentially led to do it. In view of all the circumstances, the supposition that Joseph had this large family of young children before his marriage with Mary, is so unreasonable that one may safely say it would never have had any credence in the Church but for the supposed necessity of holding, at any cost of consistency, to the non-parentage life of

Joseph and Mary. There is nothing like blind devotion to Church traditions to override reason and common sense.

This does not exhaust the catalogue of conjectures, which have had more or less of patronage from age to age in the past, all designed to furnish a mother for the "brethren" of our Savior, without allowing them to be the children of Joseph and Mary, which ought to be the most natural and honorable conclusion one could reach from the Scripture narratives. A false estimate of Paul's commendation of celibacy for the period of persecution, as an expediency in the time of the wonderful distress to which the Church was subjected, has been carried to such extremes that the estate of singleness has been exalted into a virtue, while matrimony has been disparaged as incompatible with the highest spirituality. This persistent effort, in one way or another, to make the brethren of Jesus his cousins, has brought out the conjecture that Joseph and Cleopas, or Alpheus, were brothers, and that therefore, in the popular thought, the children of the latter were related to the son of Mary in this roundabout way, which was enough to justify the evangelists in calling them "his brethren." Some ancient writers believed this relation existed between Joseph and Alpheus. We do not know whether it did or not; but whether the conjecture be true or false, it is not sufficiently authenticated to command belief; and, if believed, it does not account for the assumed fact that the children of Alpheus lived with Joseph and Mary, passing for their children, and did not live with their own parents. The ingenuity of men has not yet proved keen enough to invent an hypothesis that will satisfy all the conditions of this problem. The stubborn fact remains that in the household of the carpenter of Nazareth, there were several children living as in the home of their parents, known to the neighbors as the children of Joseph and Mary, and definitely recognized in the Scriptures as the brothers and sisters of Jesus, and never as his cousins.

It is known that one of this family was named James, and it has always been claimed by those who deny that Mary had any other child than Jesus, that this James was one of the twelve, James the Less, the son of Alpheus; and that this particular James was also the one whom the Apostle Paul recognized as "James the Lord's brother." Now, if this James was indeed James the Less, the son of Alpheus, he was not at home in Nazareth with the carpenter when Jesus came there to preach in the synagogue; when the neighbors referred to him by name as the brother of Jesus, and as at home, known to them all. James the Less, the son of Alpheus, had been called into the apostolic family before this, and was with the twelve, spending his time with them traveling about the villages and cities of Galilee, but most of the time in the vicinity of the lake of Galilee. How could he be at home and abroad at once? How could he be with the Master and the twelve, and yet with the carpenter in Nazareth? These points will become more and more significant as we proceed.

When Jesus was in the very height of his busiest journeyings from place to place, teaching and preaching, and doing wonderful works, with his twelve disciples, and large crowds waiting upon his ministry, his mother and his brethren came to see him, and wished to speak with him. They could not approach him because of the crowd. It was doubtless some important matter, either with reference to himself or the family, in which they sought to interest him. What it was is not important to us. Of their coming Matthew says: "While he yet talked to the people, behold, his mother and his brethren stood without, desiring to speak with him. Then one said unto him, Behold, thy mother and thy brethren stand without, desiring to speak with thee. But he answered and said unto him that told him, Who is my mother? and who are my brethren? And he stretched forth his hand toward his disciples, and said, Behold my mother and my brethren! For whosoever shall do the will of my Father which is in heaven, the same is my brother, and sister, and mother." (Matthew xii, 46-50. See, also, Mark iii, 31-35; and Luke viii, 19-21.) In these passages, while he sought to impress the people that the spiritual relation to God and to one another, was more valuable in the religious sense than the ties of nature, he did not disparage the latter, nor deny that the parties standing without were what they were supposed to be—"his mother and his brethren." He never denied the relation which the people thought to exist between himself and "his brethren." If the people were believing what was untrue, he confirmed them in the wrong impression, and misled them. He pointed to the most endearing relations of human life, as understood by all present, to illustrate the spiritual union between himself and those who do the will of God. If some one says he did not acknowledge "his brethren" as being such, the reply is that he treated his "mother" precisely as he did "his brethren." There is not room for doubt that all who heard him believed that his brethren were brothers indeed, the sons of his mother, and he said no word to indicate the contrary.

Beyond this, however, is the fact that at the time of this interview, while "his mother and his brethren" were without, James the Less was not with those without, but he was with the disciples within, he being one of the twelve. It is, therefore, impossible to regard him as the James whose name heads the list of "his brethren." He was not of that family, whether he was in any sense a cousin, or other relative, or not. True, it is not said that all his brethren were without, or that every member of the family was there, but the scope of the passage is entirely inconsistent with the idea that one of "his brethren" was inside with him, and had been with him from the beginning, as one of the twelve. No one would ever infer such a thing from this passage, or from any other Scripture. Every effort to make out that James the Less, the son of Alpheus, was of the family of Joseph the carpenter, and known in Nazareth, or among the twelve, or by any person on the earth, as one of "his brethren," must fail utterly, because there is nothing to support it, and very much against it. He was the son of another Mary, the wife of Cleopas, who, as has been seen, was a living disciple till after Christ's resurrection, and, without reasonable doubt, was the head of his own family, of which James the Less was a member, whether he lived in Nazareth or not; for the place of his residence is not reported in the Scriptures. From all allusions made to Nazareth, and the treatment Jesus himself received there, no one would ever suspect that one or two of the twelve apostles came from there, at so early a period as that at which he called the twelve, and ordained them apostles.

The residence of several of the apostles is given, with such distinguishing remarks concerning their families, that if one came from Nazareth, and from the family of Joseph, it is incredible that such a fact would have been passed over in silence. "Now Philip was of Bethsaida, the city of Andrew and Peter." James and John, the sons of Zebedee, are easily located. The other James was "the son of Alpheus." If Alpheus was well known, which is probable, that designation would fully identify this James, and prevent any one from thinking him of the family of Joseph of Nazareth. If Alpheus and Cleopas were the same person, Cleopas being a disciple, but not an apostle, and being the husband of "the other Mary," the family is amply identified. If Alpheus and Cleopas were not the same, the only rational conclusion is that Alpheus was the former husband of Mary, who was now the wife of Cleopas, and the mother of James. She was also the mother of Joses, who was doubtless a disciple, as his name appears in such intimate association with that of James and his mother at the crucifixion. Still another of this family came into the apostolic office, Judas the brother of James, who was one of the twelve, thought by many to be the person who was called Thaddeus by Matthew. The identity of this Judas with Thaddeus is important here only as showing that two sons of "the other Mary" were apostles early, while as yet all "his brethren" were out of the fold, and not so much as disciples. It is thought that this Judas, the brother of James, was called Thaddeus to distinguish him from the other Judas, who was also one of the twelve; that is, Judas Iscariot. But, even if this identification should fail, there is still a possibility of finding harmony as to the lists of the apostles, and a place for this Judas. When Jesus had spoken some truths too deep for the people, it is said that from that time "many of his disciples went back, and walked no more with him." They may not have apostatized, but withdrew from public identification with him. There is no hint that one of the twelve withdrew, but the Master's pathetic appeal to those that remained, indicates some apprehension as to the stability of all of them. "Then said Jesus unto the twelve, Will ye also go away? Then Simon Peter answered him, Lord, to whom shall we go? thou hast the words of eternal life." In the list of apostles as first chosen, Matthew gives the name of Lebbeus, also called Thaddeus, and only one Judas; but in the later lists, and notably that given of the eleven after the resurrection, Judas, the brother of James, appears, and Thaddeus does not. Either Thaddeus and this Judas were the same, or else Thaddeus withdrew and Judas took his place. Whether Judas, the brother of James, came into the apostolic office at the beginning as Thaddeus or not, he is in it, and one of the twelve, before any of the brethren of Jesus became believers. He, with James the Less, belonged to the other family, as has been abundantly shown, and not to the family of Joseph, the carpenter of Nazareth. When he wrote the epistle which bears his name, he called himself "Jude, the servant of Jesus Christ, and brother of James." Thus two of the family of "the other Mary" are apostles, and Joses is undoubtedly a disciple, while the fourth, Simon, may or may not have been. These can not be the brethren of Jesus, notwithstanding the similarity of their names. It is inconceivable that they should be when all the facts are taken into the account. The coincidence of names is remarkable, but that is all. There is no Scriptural authority for calling them "cousins." Their mother was one of the noblest of women, ever true to her faith, and courageous to the last degree; standing in sight of the cross, last at the tomb to see the dead body of Jesus laid away, and with the first to return at dawn of the first day of the week with spices for the anointing; then to become one of the first to be assured of his resurrection and to bear the news to his disciples. Nothing is taken from the honor of her loyalty and genuineness as a worthy disciple, and as the mother of two of the chosen twelve, by insisting that she was not the mother of those "brethren" who did not believe in Jesus during all the period of his Galilean ministry. Her sons were in the faith very early, and endured to the end; but neither of them was "James, the Lord's brother."

Chapter VI.

HIS BRETHREN NOT DISCIPLES.

THIS brings us to another fact full of significance in this discussion, and which, added to the foregoing, ought to be decisive, and settle the entire question beyond dispute. It is that "his brethren" did not believe on him, and never became disciples till after his crucifixion. The scope of the testimony is to the effect that his brethren stood together in their relations with him; and it is not improbable that his mother hesitated, and moved very slowly in committing herself to his movements, being amazed and full of wonder, not knowing whereunto his strange career would lead. She carried a burden in her heart with reference to him; for, no doubt, the prophetic words of Simeon, which fell upon her ears in the temple, often came to her with thrilling vividness, sometimes bringing a pang, and casting a shadow upon her hopes as to his future: "Yea, a sword shall pierce through thy own soul also." Her relation to him was peculiar. As yet she could only "ponder in her heart" the things she knew, and wait. But there was no division among his brethren. Neither one nor two of them became his disciples in his early ministry. They tarried with his mother while he went forth with the twelve. They were not of the twelve; therefore they were not the children of "the other Mary." Two of her children were of the twelve—James and Judas.

His standing in his own family, among his kin, and in his own house, was singular, and yet, perhaps, not unnatural. There could have been no lack of reverence on his part towards Joseph and his mother, nor of brotherly affection towards his brethren and sisters; but the mysterious outgivings of his life, which they witnessed and yet could not understand, must have tended to keep them somewhat aloof from him, and to inspire in them feelings of anxiety, if not questionings of his sanity. Indeed, his friends or kinsfolk—no doubt including his brethren—in the midst of his success, "went out to lay hold on him; for they said, He is beside himself." (Mark iii, 21.) The whole tenor of his life was beyond their comprehension. They stood in awe of him; and while they did not commit themselves to him as disciples, they did not lose brotherly regard for him. On the other hand, their backwardness to enter into full sympathy with him, must have been to him the source of keen regret. There is an evident tinge of sadness in his words when he speaks of his non-acceptance at home, although there is not lacking a strain of rebuke: "And he went out from thence, and came into his own country; and his disciples follow him. And when the Sabbath-day was come, he began to teach in the synagogue: and many hearing him were astonished, saying, From whence hath this man these things? and what wisdom is this which is given unto him, that even such mighty works are wrought by his hands? Is not this the carpenter, the son of Mary, the brother of James, and Joses, and of Judas, and Simon? and are not his sisters here with us? And they were offended in him. But Jesus said unto them, A prophet is not without honor, but in his own country, and among his own kin, and in his own house. And he could there do no mighty work, save that he laid his hands upon a few sick folk, and healed them. And he marveled because of their unbelief." (Mark vi, 1-6. See also Matt. xiii, 54-58; and Luke iv, 16-23.) In Matthew the question is: "Is not this the carpenter's son?" This is doubtless the visit to Nazareth, "where he was brought up," when the people first "wondered at the gracious words which proceeded out of his mouth," and then became angry, and "rose up, and thrust him out of the city, and led him unto the brow of the hill whereon their city was built, that they might cast him down headlong." Their sudden revulsion of feeling, seemingly caused by his intimation that God had thoughts of mercy towards some who were not Jews, shows their excitableness, as well as the strength of their bigotry as Jews. From this time forward he made Capernaum his home, and the center of his operations, probably accepting the hospitality of his aunt, the mother of Zebedee's children.

The unbelief at Nazareth, at which he marveled, was plainly painful to him. Some of his own family were implicated. This fact gave poignancy to his grief. There is pathos in the way he came, in his reply, to those who were so dear to him, and who withheld from him the confidence he craved: "Save in his own *country*, and among his own *kin*, and in his *own house*." Passing from his countrymen to his *kin*, and from his *kin* to those of his *own house*, he touched a chord that, in his mother's breast, must have awakened memories of early prophecies and deepest solicitude, and should have brought from "his brethren" responses of fraternal sympathy. With what emotions they received the expressions of his sorrow is not known; but they did not become his disciples. Neither James nor Joses nor Judas nor Simon was ready to receive his testimony, or enter into his work; much less was either ready to become an apostle. The James who was with him—James the Less—was evidently not of his *kin*, or of his *own house*. Surely this is demonstrated.

The unbelief of his brethren continued throughout his ministry in Galilee, and till after his crucifixion at Jerusalem. It was late in his ministry, and not long before his last journey to Jerusalem, when they urged him to go into Judea that his disciples might see his works, rather implying inconsistency on his part in keeping his works secret, and yet desiring public recognition of his claims. So we read: "Now the Jews' feast of tabernacles was at hand. His brethren therefore said unto him, Depart hence, and go into Judea, that thy disciples also may see the works that thou doest:

for there is no man that doeth anything in secret, and he himself seeketh to be known openly. If thou do these things, show thyself to the world. For neither did his brethren believe in him. Then Jesus said unto them, My time is not yet come: but your time is always ready. The world can not hate you: but me it hateth, because I testify of it that the works thereof are evil. Go ye up unto this feast: I go not up yet unto this feast; for my time is not yet full come. When he had said these words unto them, he abode still in Galilee. But when his brethren were gone up, then went he also up unto the feast, not openly, but as it were in secret." (John vii, 2–10.)

Evidently "his brethren" were perplexed, and while unwilling to acknowledge him as the Messiah, they were impressed with his extraordinary character.

They knew that strange influences attended him; that he did things which other men could not do; that his wisdom was beyond their depth; that the purity of his life lifted him above the suspicion of pretentiousness; that neither sordid nor selfish motives actuated him,—yet they could not realize that the long-expected King of Israel dwelt in their humble home. They were persuaded that he was no ordinary person, and were solicitous that those at Jerusalem, whom they supposed most capable, might have the opportunity, if it were possible, to discover the secret of his power. It is not unlikely that indignation sometimes mingled with their wonder, as they sought to know more of the mystery that surrounded him, only to find themselves unable to approach the solution. They naturally held him at a distance, till he became, in feeling and in fact, a "stranger to his brethren, and an alien to his mother's children."

This exact condition of things was foretold in the Psalms, proving at once the prophetic character of the Psalm as truly Messianic, and the relation of "his brethren" to himself and to his mother. In this investigation great weight is to be recognized in these prophetic utterances. They are quoted and applied to him by the evangelists so as to show their meaning and literal fulfillment. In Psalm lxix, 8, 9, we read words which the New Testament ascribes to him: "I am become a stranger unto my brethren, and an alien unto my mother's children. For the zeal of thine house hath eaten me up: and the reproaches of them that reproach thee are fallen upon me." If these words relate to Christ, their testimony is as if he had uttered them with his own lips; and their exact description of the state of things in his own household at Nazareth is something to think about.

That the language does refer to him, and is so applied in the New Testament, is unquestionable. Take the following: "And his disciples remembered that it was written, The zeal of thine house hath eaten me up." (John ii, 17.) This application to him of this sentence carries with it the application of the whole passage. The Apostle Paul applies the same passage to Christ, quoting another part of it: "For even Christ pleased not himself; but, as it is written, The reproaches of them that reproached thee fell on me." (Romans xv, 2.) Then, how pertinent and discriminating these words: "A stranger unto my brethren, and an alien unto my mother's children!" An alien, not to my kindred, nor to my cousins, nor to my father's children, but "an alien unto my mother's children"—literally, "the sons of my mother." Further along in this Psalm are other predictions concerning him, which were fulfilled in him, and were applied to him in the New Testament, confirming the interpretation which makes him and his brethren, who did not believe in him, the subjects of this prophecy: "They gave me also gall for my meat, and in my thirst they gave me vinegar to drink." (Psalm lxix, 21.) Who doubts that this was fulfilled when Jesus hung upon the cross? We read, Matthew xxvii, 34: "They gave him vinegar to drink, mingled with gall." Mark xv, 36: "And one ran and filled a sponge full of vinegar, and put it on a reed, and gave him to drink." John xix, 29: "Now there was a vessel full of vinegar, and they filled a sponge full of vinegar, and put it upon hyssop, and put it to his mouth." It can not be that any one who believes the Scriptures will doubt that the predictions of this Psalm, even in their minuteness of detail, were applied to Christ, and fulfilled in him. But, if so, here are words which belong to him, with all their significance: "I am become a stranger unto my brethren, and an alien unto my mother's children."

There are predictions in another Psalm concerning him, which were as literally fulfilled in him, and are as distinctly applied to him, which are so used by the evangelists as to corroborate the above. Psalm xxii, 15-18: "My strength is dried up like a potsherd; and my tongue cleaveth to my jaws; and thou hast brought me into the dust of death. For dogs have compassed me: the assembly of the wicked have inclosed me: they pierced my hands and my feet. I may tell all my bones: they look and stare upon me. They part my garments among them, and cast lots upon my vesture." Matthew so blends this passage in its fulfillment, with the words above quoted from Psalm lx, 19, that the two prophecies must apply alike to the same person: "They gave him vinegar to drink, mingled with gall: and when he had tasted thereof, he would not drink. And they crucified him, and parted his garments, casting lots: that it might be fulfilled which was spoken by the prophet, They parted my garments among them, and upon my vesture did they cast lots."

In the light of these prophecies, and of their fulfillment in the person of the Son of Mary, and their authoritative application to him by New Testament writers, we may well ask, What is lacking in the proof that "his brethren," who did not believe in him; who took him to be beside himself; who virtually challenged him to submit his claims to the specialists and experts of Jerusalem; and to whom he became a "stranger" and an "alien," were his mother's children? They were persistently called his brethren, not only by their neighbors, but by his disciples and by the evangelists, and this till after his crucifixion and ascension; and finally, by the Apostle Paul after their conversion. Not one of them was of "the twelve," but they are always distinguished from "the twelve," so that they can not be confounded with the children of the other Mary without absolute confusion.

Possibly this attitude of his brethren towards him may help us to understand some things in his earthly life, and especially in his course towards his family, that some have thought strange. It is evident that he did not seem to value the ties of flesh and blood as many others do. He looked upon them in the light of higher relationships in the kingdom of God, which were constantly before his mind, and the contrast brought worldly things to their proper level. His constant exaltation of the spiritual above the temporal is the explanation of what appears to be a disregard of the claims of these earthly relationships. He is not known to have shown any partiality towards his brethren, because they were his brethren; nor to have made any excuse for their unbelief on this account. So, also, in his relation to his mother, while he was kind and courteous and affectionate, yet he sometimes appeared stern and almost disrespectful.

At the time of his visit to Jerusalem, at twelve years of age, this peculiarity exhibited itself. He tarried behind when his parents started home, without consulting them. When they missed him, and returned and found him, with great tenderness his mother referred to the anxiety they had felt while seeking him "sorrowing." In his reply we have the first recorded words from his lips. In them there is no expression of regret for their trouble or sorrow, but what approaches the character of rebuke. "And he said unto them, How is it that ye sought me? Wist ye not that I must be about my Father's business?" He saw, as they did not, the higher claims of the things of God. When at the marriage at Cana, where his mother was active,* and probably anticipated a miracle, he displayed a disposition not to permit any one, not even his mother, to meddle with what was his own work. When the wine was exhausted, his

---

* Some think one of her daughters was the bride.

mother came and said to him, "They have no wine!" "Jesus said unto her, Woman, what have I to do with thee? Mine hour is not yet come." These words can hardly be explained without including in their meaning some elements of rebuke. It was not dislike to his mother, or to womanhood, but his unyielding purpose not to permit interference with his own work, or to allow any worldly influence or motive to sway him in what pertained to his mission. When his mother and his brethren came where he was teaching, and wanted to speak with him, he did not deny their relation to him, nor their claim upon his attention; but he took occasion to show his higher appreciation of the spiritual relation that grows out of obedience to God, and membership in the kingdom of heaven.

In all these instances he shows that

the spiritual and eternal have precedence over the material and temporal relations. The lesson was taught by his action more impressively than it could be by words. It is the lesson taught in his terms of discipleship, when he requires that father, mother, wife, children, and all possessions be given up, or held in abeyance, so as not to stand in the way of complete devotion to his service. "Whosoever loveth father or mother more than me, is not worthy of me." On this high plane he lived on earth, never hesitating, never faltering in any emergency, and never failing to make the will of God the supreme law of his life and being. Even his mother could not fully understand him, and to his brethren he was a perplexity and grief. They could not enter into his sphere, nor realize the power of his consecration; so they waited, and wondered, and wished him to go to Jerusalem, the seat of wisdom and knowledge, that his claims to the supernatural might be tested. His brethren did not believe. His standard was too high for them till after the dispensation of the Spirit came with power.

Chapter VII.

HIS BRETHREN CONVERTED.

AFTER this study of the attitude of the family of Mary towards her first-born son, and the recognition of their persistent doubts, it is a comfort to be assured that at last "his brethren" were all brought into the kingdom of God and numbered with the saved.

The details of their conversion are not available. The exact time of the abandonment of their doubts, and of the opening of their hearts to the testimony that satisfied them, we may not know; nor can we trace their mental processes in entering into the faith; but the very brief recognition of their discipleship with which we are favored points pretty conclusively to their acceptance of the proofs of his resurrection from the dead, and joining themselves to the company of believers as a result. Before his last journey to Jerusalem, and, as far as we can gather, up to the time of the crucifixion, they held themselves apart, and formed a distinct company in all their movements. They are always separately classed, as in John ii, 12: "After this he went down to Capernaum, he, and his mother, and his brethren, and his disciples; and they continued there not many days." This was not the removal of the family, but was a family visit, possibly to the home of her sister. When he was within, with the twelve, his mother and his brethren stood without. They were interested enough in him and in his work to look after him; and their faithful attendance upon their mother in all her movements is worthy of admiration. With such a mother and such surroundings, it must be that they possessed some admirable traits of character. They were, no doubt, model young men, such as Jesus loved, as was the young man of the Gospel who wanted to know what good thing he should do in order to inherit eternal life. In all the Scriptural references to them and their course with regard to Jesus, there is no intimation of misconduct, or of undutiful action towards their parents, or even towards their elder brother, except the fact that they did not become his disciples.

They observed the requirements of the law, and went up to the feasts at Jerusalem, as they had done from their youth. When the Feast of Tabernacles was approaching, as we have seen, they urged Jesus to go to it, and show himself to the world. It can not be doubted that they were at Jerusalem at the time of his arrest. Their loyalty to their mother, and his, would keep them near her person. They could not fail to be anxious observers of all that was taking place. We must suppose that they were present at his trial; that they saw the confusion of Pilate; that they heard the shout of the rabble, crying, "Away with him! crucify him!" and without doubt they followed to Golgotha, and kept with his other acquaintances from Galilee, who stood afar off, and beheld these things. They joined their mother and her relatives, who were present, in mourning his tragic end. Nor is it at all unlikely that they saw his body taken from the cross and laid in Joseph's new tomb. On the first day of the week they were not far away when the news of his rising spread abroad. Strange if they did not visit the empty sepulcher! Soon they heard the witnesses tell their story, who had seen him alive. At some point or other, while these stirring events were taking place, their doubts gave way, and the light and joy of faith dawned upon their souls, as they realized the fact that he had risen. They humbly accepted the testimony that proved him divine. Step by step they followed on till they saw him for themselves, and knew that he lived again. Tarrying still in Jerusalem, and companying with his friends from Galilee, they learned all. If they went to Galilee, they probably saw him in the mountain, and mingled with the large company when five hundred saw him at once. They were back in Jerusalem before he was taken up, and from the Mount of Olivet they gazed at his ascending form till the cloud received him out of their sight. Then, too, they must have heard the words of the angel, saying: "Ye men of Galilee, why stand ye gazing up into heaven? this same Jesus, which is taken up from you into heaven, shall so come in like manner as ye have seen him go into heaven." From this sight, and from this angelic testimony, they gladly returned to Jerusalem, their souls enraptured with triumphant faith, and were henceforth numbered with the disciples.

This is not all fancy. The record which discloses this outcome is unequivocal. When the celestial visitors of the ascension escort, who tarried behind, had delivered their greeting and message to the "men of Galilee," it is said of the company of believers: "Then returned they unto Jerusalem from the mount called Olivet, which is from Jerusalem a Sabbath-day's journey. And when they were come in, they went up into an upper room, where abode both Peter, and James, and John, and Andrew, Philip, and Thomas, Bartholomew, and Matthew, James the son of Alpheus, and Simon Zelotes, and Judas the brother of James. These all continued with one accord in prayer and supplication, with the women, and Mary the mother of Jesus, and with his brethren." (Acts i, 12-14.) Here are all the apostles, including James the son of Zebedee, and James the son of Alpheus, and Judas the brother of James, and the women, and Mary the mother of Jesus, *and his brethren!* His brethren are not included in the list of the apostles. Not one of them as yet belongs to that company. James and Judas, the two sons of "the other Mary," are in that list, but "his brethren" are not. Yet now at length they are with the disciples, *for the first time.* Their unbelief is gone, and from the Mount of Olivet they come with the company of believers into this "upper room," and henceforth they are in the inner circle of this holy fellowship. "The number of names together were about one hundred and twenty," and "his brethren," the sons of his mother, are all within. They, with the others, await the promise of the Father, and share the baptism of Pentecost. On them was poured out the gift of the Holy Ghost. Their induction into the kingdom was complete.

In after years the Apostle Paul recognizes them as standing high in the Church. He was not of "the twelve," and his apostleship was challenged by some, to which challenge he gave answer: "If I be not an apostle to others, yet doubtless I am to you: for the seal of mine apostleship are ye in the Lord. Mine answer to them that do examine me is this: Have we not power to eat and to drink? Have we not power to lead about a sister, a wife, as well as other apostles, and as the brethren of the Lord, and Cephas? Or I only and Barnabas, have not we power to forbear working?" He and Barnabas had been working with their hands to support themselves, and had appeared to some not quite up to the standard of apostleship, and Paul shows why they did it. Their service in this regard was voluntary. They fully appreciated their right to "forbear working," and to become a charge to the Church; to avail themselves of all domestic privileges and comforts; to marry, and gather about them the advantages of home,—as "the brethren of the Lord" had done, without reproach, and as Cephas or Peter had done. "Even so hath the Lord ordained that they which preach the gospel should live of the gospel. But I have used none of these things. . . .

For it were better for me to die, than that any man should make my glorying void. . . . What is my reward then? Verily that, when I preach the gospel, I may make the gospel of Christ without charge, that I abuse not my power in the gospel." In this way Paul justified himself in continuing without a wife; at the same time claiming the same rights in this respect that were enjoyed by Peter and "the brethren of the Lord." Surely, then, these "brethren" had become eminent in the Church of God, worthy to be cited as examples in connection with the apostles.

It was not because he deemed it unlawful for him to have a wife; for he claimed the right, and vindicated it, showing that his commendation of celibacy was only for times of persecution, and that his practice of it was voluntary, and simply a matter of expediency. He would not burden the Church with his own support, much less just then with the support of himself with a family. In support of his right to marry, he pointed to the example of Peter, who was known to be a married man; and in this connection he referred, in a general way, to "the other apostles," without naming them, but so as to imply that some of them were married. It is not known whether John was or not. When he took Mary, the mother of Jesus, to "his own home" to live, he either took her to his mother's house, which was yet his home, as before stated, or else he was married, and had a home of his own. Paul also alludes to "the brethren of the Lord," who were doubtless by this time highly esteemed and influential in the Church, and some of them, at least, married. This allusion to "the brethren of the Lord," as honored disciples, can not be misunderstood. They were yet distinct from "the twelve," but they were believers, well known, and worthy to be cited as examples.

The oldest of these "brethren of the Lord" was James; at least his name is first in the list given by the evangelists. He, like Paul and Barnabas, was not of "the twelve." There were, however, two of the name in the original twelve— the son of Zebedee, and the son of Alpheus. It is clear that there were other apostles besides the twelve, for Paul and Barnabas were such. At some time after the Pentecost another James became an apostle, and was known to Paul as "James the Lord's brother." This distinguished him from James the brother of John, and from James the son of Alpheus and brother of Jude; but it does not entitle him to all the honor which tradition has given him. In the early ages of the Church, the "fathers" spoke of him as James the Just, as the first Bishop of Jerusalem, as presiding in the council at Jerusalem, and as doing many things which were really done by James the Less.

Chapter VIII.

"THE LORD'S BROTHER."

THE date at which Paul visited Jerusalem, when he saw "James the Lord's brother," is not easily fixed. It was after his conversion, and after he had been in Arabia, and had returned to Damascus. Whether the three years he mentions included all the time of his absence from Jerusalem, since he started to Damascus on his mission of persecution, till he returned to see Peter; or whether it was three years after he returned from Arabia to Damascus, before he went to Jerusalem, is an open question. It is thought by some that he went to Jerusalem immediately after his escape from Damascus, when he was let down from the wall in a basket; but his own account does not look that way. He was evidently absent from Jerusalem three years. His visit to see Peter may have been a private visit, for his personal benefit, before he went to Tarsus, where he was subsequently found by Barnabas, and taken over to Antioch, and put into active service.

A close inspection of the record indicates that after his conversion, and first preaching in Damascus, and his escape therefrom, Paul was not known as an active apostle for some considerable time; perhaps not till after the great revival in Antioch, the news of which came to the Church in Jerusalem, and caused that Church to send Barnabas to Antioch to see about it. Barnabas went and inspected the work, and approved it, and joined in to help it along. He had not been there long till he felt the need of more help, and went to Antioch to seek Paul. The account in Acts ix reads as if Paul came directly to Jerusalem from Damascus; but this account does not give dates, and this visit must have been after he had been in Arabia. It may have been his visit to Jerusalem when he essayed to join himself to the disciples, and they were afraid of him, and would not believe he was a disciple. "Then Barnabas took him and brought him to the apostles, and declared unto them how he had seen the Lord in the way, and that he had spoken to him, and how he had preached boldly in Damascus in the name of Jesus." This was not a private visit to Peter; for he was with the apostles, coming in and going out, and spake boldly in the name of the Lord Jesus, and disputed with the Grecians. If this was the occasion when he saw only Peter and James the Lord's brother, it must have been before Barnabas became an apostle; for he saw Barnabas, and Barnabas took him to the apostles, and attested his conversion and discipleship. This was probably a short visit, and immediately after it, Paul was taken by the brethren to Cesarea, and went on to Tarsus. It may be that at that time the other apostles were all out of the city, so that only Peter and this James were there. Paul himself was a disciple, but not yet accredited as an apostle. This was also the standing of Barnabas at that time; but after the great work at Antioch, both Barnabas and Paul became apostles, and went forth fully equipped for all of the work of apostles. Barnabas, after introducing Paul in Jerusalem, and vouching for his discipleship, was sent to Antioch, and thence went to Tarsus, and found Paul; and the two together continued there a year, and after visiting other places, doing evangelistic work, they were together sent to Jerusalem with the contributions of the Churches for the poor in Judea. These two were specially set apart at Antioch, and ordained apostles, under the direction of the Holy Ghost, and sent forth by the Church to their special work; and this after they had returned from their mission of charity to Jerusalem. From which it appears that apostles could be made by the Church without the presence of other apostles, and without the formality of an appointment or approval by the apostles, or by the Mother Church in Jerusalem. It is possible that Paul's first visit to Jerusalem to see Peter was while the elder James was yet living. If so, he was not in the city at the time, or Paul would have seen him. After the persecution that arose about Stephen, which appears to have been quite a while after the death of Stephen, those of prominence in the Church, doubtless including several apostles, "were scattered abroad," and went to Phenice and Cyprus and Antioch, preaching the Word. Through their instrumentality the work was begun in Antioch. It was almost certainly during the time of this "scattering abroad," or while the apostles were engaged in the work begun at that time in distant parts, that Paul came and found so few apostles in Jerusalem.

Peter was there, and so was "James the Lord's brother." It is not unlikely that the latter was as yet quite young in the office. Paul himself had not entered it. He was a disciple, and had preached in Damascus, but was not yet accredited as he was after his labors in Antioch, and his ordination there. Whether any other James was in the city or not, when Paul, years afterward, wrote of this visit, he applied the descriptive phrase to the one he saw, so as to distinguish him from both the others of the name, who were apostles from the beginning. If Josephus confounded this James with James the Less, and spoke of the Lord's brother when he meant James the Less, he made a very natural mistake, such as others made, and have been making through all these centuries. But Paul made no mistake of this kind. He spoke of James the Less in the same epistle, but applied no descriptive epithet to him. He was the James whom Peter feared, and because of whom he "dissembled." Before that time the elder James had been killed with the sword, and previous to this execution James the Less had always been so designated; but now he is simply James. "Go tell James;" "came from James;" "after they all held their peace, James answered." These expressions show how this James now stood. He needed no other description; but another James, younger than he, just admitted to the office, must be distinguished. He is "James the Lord's brother." At whatever time this third James became an apostle, whether before or after the death of the first James, some descriptive title was necessary, in order to avoid confusion; and no other was so natural or expressive as the one Paul used. It was the one he had always borne, was well understood, and distinguished him from both the others.

That this third James became an apostle, seems the necessary conclusion from all that has gone before. It has been clearly shown that the son of Alpheus was not a cousin to Jesus; never lived with Mary his mother, and was one of "the twelve" when James and

Joses and Simon and Judas were all at home in Nazareth, known as "his brethren." The other Mary was not the sister of his mother; but her sons were disciples, and two of them apostles, before "his brethren" believed on him. These facts, so clearly proven, leave us no alternative. "James the Lord's brother" must have been the James who was known in Nazareth long after the twelve were chosen and ordained, and who did not become a disciple till after the resurrection. This phrase, "the brethren of the Lord," was kept up too persistently not to have had a basis and reason in actual fact.

No trustworthy account of the apostolic labors of this third James has come down to us. The same is true with regard to the labors of several of the others who were apostles from the beginning. We can not tell where they lived, whither they went, or where they died. Vague traditions are all we have, but our ignorance does not discredit their apostleship. Neither should it that of the third James. Early Church history tells what the fathers of the early centuries thought and believed with regard to several of whom we know so little, and also of this "James the Lord's brother;" but it is next to impossible to distinguish between what was ascribed to James the Less, and to this third James; for at that early day the habit of speaking of James the Less as James the Just and "James the Lord's brother," was becoming common.

There is nothing in the slightest degree unreasonable in the claim that one of "his brethren," who lived in the home of his mother, and was reared under her care, and yet so long withstood the evidences of his Messiahship, and only consented to become a disciple after the most indubitable proofs of his resurrection from the dead, should at last become an apostle of Christ. His eligibility and qualifications were complete. He was an "eye-witness" of the death and resurrection, in that he saw him after he was alive from the dead; and there is no doubt that he saw him ascend from Mount Olivet, and heard the voice of the angel, and returned with joy to the city, and shared the enduement of power in the upper room, receiving the baptism of the Holy Ghost on the day of Pentecost. What, then, was lacking to make him an apostle indeed? In natural ability and moral fitness he was equal to the demand. He was probably the peer of any of the twelve. Being the oldest of the family, next to "the first-born son" of Mary, he was now about the age that Jesus was when he began his ministry. Why should he not become an apostle? He was, indeed, "James the Lord's brother."

The question has arisen as to the number of the apostles. It is held that there could be only twelve. The impression prevailed among the apostles themselves at the start, that twelve was the fixed number. When Judas fell, they thought they must fill his place from amongst those who were eyewitnesses, and could give testimony to the resurrection. Whether this were necessary or not, they so regarded it. But others became apostles afterwards. Whether more than twelve were in the office at one time, does not appear. Possibly not. Paul and Barnabas became apostles in the fullest sense. It may be that some died before this occurred. That is not important. It may be that the first James was killed with the sword before the third James came into the apostleship. This is not impossible. We only know that Paul saw him, and declared him an apostle, and called him "James the Lord's brother."

Others did much apostolic work, and joined with Paul in some of his apostolic epistles. Timothy, Sylvanus, and Sosthenes did this. Apollos and Silas were active and successful ministers, and so were Luke and Mark; but whether they were ever inducted into the office as apostles is not known. Apollos was closely identified with the office in Paul's writings, and perhaps not less in the work he did. He appears nearly on a level with the great apostle himself when Paul says: "For while one saith, I am of Paul; and another, I am of Apollos, are ye not carnal? Who then is Paul, and who is Apollos, but ministers by whom ye believed?" "I have planted, and Apollos watered; but God gave the increase." Again: "All things are yours; whether Paul, or Apollos, or Cephas, or the world." Surely, if Apollos was not an apostle, he was little inferior in position or power.

Perhaps he lacked one thing. It seems to have been necessary to the office that the incumbent should have seen the Lord after his resurrection. Paul was not an exception to this requirement, for he says: "And last of all he was seen of me also, as of one born out of due time." (1 Corinthians xv, 8.) If this was indispensable, as it was evidently regarded, it did not exclude "James the Lord's brother," who returned from Olivet with the disciples after the ascension, and with his mother entered the upper room. He was of the one hundred and twenty. If it was necessary to the apostolate that one should be an "eyewitness to the resurrection," or should have "seen the Lord," the discontinuance of the office after the "eyewitnesses" were dead, is readily understood. The pretentious claim to successorship in this office, set up by the Roman Catholic Church, and by some Protestant Churches, proves an unfounded assumption. The only successorship that is either possible or valuable is in the spiritual functions of the gospel ministry. Whoever is called of God to the ministry of the Word, and is graciously endowed for the work by the gift of the Holy Spirit, is the true successor of the apostles. In this sense Apollos and Timothy and Silas, and many others, were apostles indeed; ministers with the apostolic spirit, doing the chiefest of all apostolic work, winning souls to Christ, and edifying the Church. This apostolic ministry abides. It is, therefore, proper to hold that any Church which is steadfast in the apostles' doctrine, and in the fellowship of the saints, holding fast the form of sound words, and maintaining the spirit of the gospel of peace, is a genuine Church of Christ, and entitled to recognition as such by all the brotherhood of believers who love our Lord Jesus Christ, and love one another with pure hearts fervently

The End.

www.ingramcontent.com/pod-product-compliance
Lightning Source LLC
Chambersburg PA
CBHW020828190426
43197CB00037B/733